Redefining Literacy for the 21st Century

David F. Warlick

Linworth
PUBLISHING, INC

Your Trusted
Library-to-Classroom Connection.
Books, Magazines, and Online

Library of Congress Cataloging-in-Publication Data

Warlick, David.
  Redefining literacy for the 21st century / by David F. Warlick.
    p. cm.
Includes bibliographical references.
  ISBN 1-58683-130-5 (pbk.)
  1. Computers and literacy. 2. Education--Effect of technological
innovations on. 3. Curriculum planning. I. Title: Redefining literacy
for the twenty-first century. II. Title.
LC149.5.W35 2004
371.33--dc22

                              2003023073

Published by Linworth Publishing, Inc.
480 East Wilson Bridge Road, Suite L
Worthington, Ohio 43085

ISBN: 1-58683-130-5

5 4 3 2 1

Table of Contents

Table of Figures

Acknowledgments

This book owes its planning and execution to more people than I can possibly mention here. So I will list only a few. First, thanks to my father, Norman Warlick, a true computer visionary. He recognized the potential of computers in the 1960s without an advanced degree in mathematics or engineering. Thanks also to my mother, who taught me to finish anything I start, and to have joy in the doing.

As with all of my writing, I thank Paul Gilster, my neighbor and author of many books on science and technology. Watch out for his new book on the future of interstellar space travel. "Tack the universe!"

A very special and loving thank you for my wife, Brenda, who had the courage to say, "Quit your job and let's have a try at consulting." In the same breath, I thank my daughter, Ryann, and son, Martin, two twenty-first century literate teenagers.

A very special thank you to Sherry York, my project manager, and Linworth Editor Donna Miller for their patience, humor, and priceless advice and encouragement—and thanks to that fateful shuttle ride from the Orlando International Airport, when Donna and I met.

One final thanks to the crew at the Lassiter Starbucks, who fueled this book with their endless African blends.

About the Author

David Warlick's unique voice and message combines a wide range of experiences, both in and outside the education arena. He ran two businesses before graduating from high school and spent more than a year in manufacturing before completing his undergraduate work. Since then he has been a middle-school teacher, central office administrator, and technology integration consultant for the North Carolina State Department of Public Instruction, where he built the nation's first state department of education Web site.

Since 1995, Mr. Warlick has been the owner and principal consultant of **The Landmark Project**, a professional development and Web design firm in Raleigh, North Carolina. During this time David has spoken at conferences and delivered workshops for educators in nearly every state of the United States and to audiences in Europe, Asia, and South America.

David lives in Raleigh, North Carolina, with his wife and two children.

Introduction and User's Guide

There has been no time in human history quite like this. Our world is changing more rapidly than ever before, and more of us are aware of these changes than ever before. The planet has never seemed so small as we witness events around the world in real time through our televisions that are connected to a global network of cables and satellite communications. At no time was this sense of a global family more obvious than the day that we entered the twenty-first century and the world watched the first celebrators in the island nation of Kiribati, the first inhabited islands west of the International Date Line. Through the following 24 hours, we all watched as each time zone marked the beginning of a new century with fireworks and celebration.

The seemingly viral spread of communication across the planet astounds us all, especially as people living in villages without running water walk around with cell phones and surf the Net with battery-powered notebook computers connected wirelessly to the World Wide Web. We are communicating with each other in ways that would have seemed pure science fiction only a few years ago, and the sheer vastness of the information that is available today through the World Wide Web boggles the mind, as do the seemly magical tools that assist us in searching for relevant information within a library of billions of documents. Advances in genetic research, nanotechnology, and explorations of the universe and the inside of an atom are causing us to redefine our existence in fundamental ways.

Examples of breakthrough discoveries and technologies could fill this book. But it is equally important to recognize that these advances are happening at a rate that renders them almost unnoticed. It was only a decade ago that we were limited to the information in our classrooms and school media centers in order to teach our children about the world around them. Today, however, we take for granted the fact that we can casually use the World Wide Web to look up spur-of-the-moment interests, important questions, reliable references, or major topics of research.

Our children seem especially immune to and oblivious of the unprecedented changes happening around us. At the same time, they seem to exemplify the new way of viewing the world through information. This is especially evident when considering the presents that children ask for at birthdays and holidays. When I was young and was asked what I wanted Santa to bring, it was model cars, airplanes, balls, bats, shoulder pads for football, science kits, erector sets, and lots of LEGOs. I almost never asked for books or magazines, which were pretty much the only formats for information available at the time.

My children, on the other hand, ask almost exclusively for information in the form of music on CDs, movies on DVDs, MP3 files, games on disk or cartridge, and the devices that play this information. They also ask for books. The only non-digital items that my son consistently requests are Lord of the Rings Trading Cards, produced by Decipher Inc. He collects the cards and arranges them into *decks* depending on each card's unique characteristics. He then takes his decks to tournaments at local book stores where he matches his decks with those of his geeky friends (and I use the descriptor *geeky* with respect and admiration) within a complex strategy game that I am frankly not educated enough to understand. Even these cards are about information.

Our children understand the premise that it is all about information. They understand the value of information and the devices that play it. They also understand communication. My daughter recently hosted a New Year's Eve party, to which she invited about 10 of her friends. As I observed the teenagers (male and female), I was amazed at how well they got along and seemed to enjoy each other's company. It was not at all like parties I attended when I was a teenager, where the pressures of romance and status weighed so heavily on me. Today, teens do not go in pairs, but in groups, and are intensely loyal to each other. They know each other because they are always together, if not physically, then virtually, as they IM in the evening and early morning. (If you do not know about IM, ask your students.)

Our job, as educators, is to prepare our students for their futures. This job today is especially challenging, because, for the first time in history, we cannot clearly describe the future for which we are preparing our children. Our world and the information that describes it are changing too quickly. The very nature of information is changing: how you find it, what it looks like, the way it behaves, where it comes from, what you can do with it, and how we, as authors, create it.

As we grapple with the changing nature of information, we must also recognize that we are working in twentieth century schools and libraries, many of them built before the advent of the personal computer—during the Industrial Age. We also seek to teach a set of standards based on a core literacy that is nearly two centuries old. The phrase *The 3Rs* was coined in 1828 by Sir William Curtis, the Lord Mayor of London. For those adept at spelling, it should come as no surprise that the Honorable Lord Mayor was, himself, illiterate.

Reconciling this convergence of twentieth century curriculum, Industrial Age schools, and the new tools and rapidly changing nature of information has been one of the major struggles of education for the past 20 years. More than any other movement, the call to Integrate Technology has symbolized our efforts to modernize our classrooms for twenty-first century teaching and learning. This book, however, will take a different approach in promoting a retooling of our classrooms. Technology should not be the goal of our reforms. To emphasize technology would result in the purchase of expensive hardware and software that solves no problems and fails to prepare our students for the future, especially as that technology would almost certainly become outdated long before student users graduate.

Large Idea!

Such is the goal of this book: to redefine literacy...

Children attend school to learn and to learn to teach themselves. We accomplish these goals with information and, as the nature of information changes, perhaps we should seek to retool our classrooms by redefining literacy—and then use technology to integrate these new basic skills. Such is the goal of this book: to redefine literacy, explore the impact that twenty-first century literacy might have on classrooms, and suggest strategies that teachers and library media specialists might adopt to begin to integrate these new skills and knowledge.

Much of this work has already been done by very smart people with the development of numerous information, digital, and technology literacy guides. These infinitely valuable documents have been developed, dispersed, and used by forward-thinking educators around the globe. Nonetheless, the core of education reform remains reading, writing, and mathematics. It is not the intent of this book to replace the 3Rs but to expand our notions of what it means to be able to read within a global electronic library of multimedia information; to use, analyze, manipulate, and add value to data that is almost exclusively digital; and to have our ideas heard in a world where messages must compete for attention among the vast amount of other information that is out there.

This is no small task, but the outcome should be small. Readers of this book should walk away with the ability to talk about a new definition of literacy very simply and convincingly in only a few sentences. By making it simple—this is how we will succeed in modernizing education.

User's Guide

There are several conventions that I will follow throughout this book in order to make it easier to use. For one, I will be emphasizing or "double-clicking" several large ideas that have given me pause and cause to rethink what I do, and what I promote in my efforts to help retool schools and classrooms for the twenty-first century. I believe that the ideas will give you something to think about and discuss with your colleagues, administrators, students, and parents. You will know when we have encountered one of these large ideas when it is repeated as a side bar in larger bolder text on the outside margin of the page.

In the early stages of planning this project, I decided not to emphasize the "how to" aspects of integrating a new literacy. Although there will be some points where I provide instructions and even diagrams, in most cases, I will urge you to seek out someone with whom you work for instructions on how to accomplish these tasks with the computers, software, and infrastructure you have in your school. Your helper may be a fellow teacher, your library media specialist, or the school's technology facilitator. It may be your district network administrator, director of technology, or even a parent. Also, do not hesitate to ask your students. It probably would not surprise you that they know more about these tools than you do, and we should profit from that fact as a point of conversation about tools, learning, and students' futures. This is actually the main reason why I suggest that you find a local expert to help you with technical instructions. It will give you and your colleague a place to talk about the need to modernize your classrooms and schools and how to go about it.

Most chapters will end with an Action Items section that suggests specific actions for library media specialists, teachers, administrators, parents, and students. If after reading the chapter you ask yourself, "What do I do now?" this section will give you practical tips that you can enact today in your classroom, media center, or school to begin to help it become a more artfully digital place.

One aspect of this book that is unique, though by no means a first, is a Web site that will be available to its readers. This Web site will serve three major purposes.

1. You will be able to access this page and view digital versions of the charts that list Web-based and other resources that could change over the months and years. I will be keeping these listings up-to-date, with your help, so that you will continue to use the ideas of this book even when the digital pages have become out-of-date.
2. Handouts and work forms that are mentioned and illustrated in this book will be available as downloads from the Web site, usually as MS Word files (.doc). You will be able to load these into your word processor, alter for your own situation, and add branding for your school or district. I do ask that you contact me to let me know how you are using these resources.

3. The Web site will serve as a meeting place. There will be an online discussion forum for each chapter in this book. Other forums will also be available for more general discussions about modernizing schools and the barriers that we must overcome. I hope that this will be a place where we can grow the ideas of this book by sharing each of our perspectives and experiences, which will make this book a more powerful tool than could be offered on any piece of paper. You can reach this Web site at <http://landmark-project.com/redefining_literacy>.

Finally, I will be telling a lot of stories in this book. Jennifer James, a cultural anthropologist in Seattle, Washington, and frequent keynote speaker at educational technology conferences, talks about leadership. She says that there are three kinds of effective leaders.

1. There is the leader who is so good at what he or she does that people are inspired to follow his or her lead and change their thinking in order to conform to this great person's accomplishments. Think of Oprah Winfrey as an example of one who leads through sheer skill.
2. There is also the leader who is so creative and effective in giving us new ways of looking at things that people want to look in the same directions, alter their perceptions, and address problems with new solutions. Albert Einstein may be an example of the leader who exhibits this characteristic.
3. Finally, there is the leader who can tell a compelling new story. A good example is Ronald Reagan. He was not exceptionally skilled, and he was not especially creative, but he told a compelling story. For better or for worse, he changed much about this country and about the world because people listened and believed him (James, 2002).

There is a story about education that we all know. It is part of the foundation of our culture, because it is the story of our own experiences from the 12 or 13 years that we all spent in classrooms listening to teachers, completing our worksheets, and cramming for tests. This story exercises enormous influence over how we teach and manage our classrooms today and the visions that our society aspires to in reforming education. We need a new story, one that represents our children, the world that they live in, and the world that they will inherit from us and shape with their own skills, knowledge, and imagination.

The first chapter of this book will be a story. This story has not happened—yet. It is a fictional tale of a school in the future and how it might look and operate. I hope that you enjoy this and other shorter stories that are included in this book as you begin to learn about and implement this new literacy in your school with your students. This is our task as educators—to tell a new story about teaching and learning in the twenty-first century and use this story to shape the teaching and learning environment.

1 Setting the Stage—
A Future Fiction

T his first chapter is a work of future fiction. I do not call it science fiction because I have every reason to expect that schools can change this much, and that it could happen during my career. If they do not, it will not be because the technology is not available, but because we did not have the courage or vision to make such dramatic changes in the way that we prepare our students for their future.

Some of what you read in this short story will seem unbelievable. However, if you are aware of the advances in computers and networking over the past 10 years, it will not be the technology that surprises you. It will more likely be what learners and educators do while they are engaged in teaching and learning. So let us remove the veil of our own Industrial Age upbringing for just a few minutes and see one possibility. Welcome to the Bacon School, 2014.

The Story

Sally Crabtree sits at her desk as her A2 students amble out of her classroom, most talking in pairs and threes, some glancing at their tablets for messages from friends, parents, or project collaborators. Sally crosses her legs, lays her tablet in her lap, and begins dragging icons around on the smooth bright surface using the stylus she slides out of the holder on the edge of the information appliance. As she busily works at her device, the information on the large plasma display at the front of the room begins to change, some sections of text and images moving around, new ones are appearing, and others are disappearing. Blocks of information slide down into view, illustrating weather conditions via Web-cams in other parts of the world. Finally, Arabic music plays, care of a Baghdad radio station.

Outside her classroom, students stroll down the halls toward their next class, B2 (B period, 2nd day of the week), or huddle in groups, talking and drawing on their tablet displays with fingers or styluses. Most of the conversations are purely the social exchanges between newly pubescent middle schoolers. However, a significant number of the discussions are about the class projects in which teams of students are constantly engaged. Projects are the primary activity of the Bacon School, and most other schools in 2014.

As she prepares for B2 to begin, Sally thinks back to her drive to school that morning with her young and excitable friend Isaac Johnson, one of the school's media center managers.

Earlier in the Morning:

Sally had just picked Isaac up at his small rental house, almost exactly halfway between her family's home and the Bacon School. She had been listening to John Grisham's latest book, which was being read to her in a Mississippi accent by her tablet. She touched the Stop icon on her tablet, as her nearly silent hybrid car glided to the curb in front of the refurbished mill house. Isaac, who had been sitting on the porch scanning the news on his tablet while sipping his customary breakfast cola, dropped his tablet into his canvas messenger bag, jumped off of the porch, and slid into the passenger seat. As Sally pulled out onto the road again, their conversation went directly to Sally's beloved Reptiles, one of her student teams. Isaac was aware that the team would be making its project presentation that morning during B2 since he worked intimately with many of the school's teams on a daily basis. Sally had especially enjoyed the Reptiles since the day at the beginning of the year when the team chose its name. It was Alf's idea, but each of the other members came up with a particular reason why the name fit.

The team was uniquely diverse in terms of academic characteristics. Two members, Desmone and Johann, were random thinkers and attention deficit. Samuel was a high achiever with an excellent memory and analytical mind. Alf remained emotionally traumatized by the unfortunate and vicious separation and divorce of his parents a year earlier. Both parents had little interest in supporting their 13-year-old son through his turmoil, each too engaged in their own bitterness and adjustment. Regardless of this odd diversity, the team had jelled into an exciting force for producing surprisingly insightful work.

Isaac described how the team had been working after classes, with Desmone and Samuel completing the text report version of the project and Johann and Alf polishing up their audiovisual. He added that just as often Alf had been working by himself on another component of the project, which remained remains a mystery.

"Finding the resources for their visuals was not a problem," Isaac said, "but validating them was a useful challenge. Each of the team members took a section of Earth history and created Web shelves in their personal information libraries with resources that they identified. They shared their Web shelves and used the information as a basis for their evaluation. It was an interesting learning experience for the team. I've asked if components of their shelves might be included in the Media Center.

"It was brilliant that we required Johann to handle the audiovisual editing and told Samuel that he could only support Johann verbally," Isaac continued, admiringly. "Frankly, I was afraid that I would be pulled into supporting Johann more than I would like, but I found that he called on Samuel at least as much as he called on me. Also, he grasped the concepts and developed his skill, and he really seemed focused on the communication, not technique."

Sally smiled at the reference to her scheme. "Thanks for supporting me on this, Isaac."

As the B2 bell rings, Isaac sits at his desk in the media center and touches icons on his tablet causing a white document to appear on the display, a diagram of the Bacon School campus. He then taps with his finger the location on the map corresponding with Ms. Crabtree's classroom. Suddenly, a full-motion, real-time video of the classroom appears on his tablet, captured by a camera that is mounted in the back of the room near the ceiling.

An additional document slides out of the video window and lists the owners of about 50 computers, which are also monitoring that classroom. There are usually five to 10 viewers of any one class, usually parents who are monitoring what their children are doing and how they are behaving. Some pop in just to learn. However, when there is going to be a team project presentation, many more parents, other residents of the community, and often teachers and students from other schools drop in to watch. All teams maintain Web sites that represent the progress of their work, including their work logs, considered resources, defenses, and their presentation dates.

As the students begin entering Mr. Johnson's classroom, Isaac thinks back to an encounter he had with Desmone this morning just before A2.

Earlier in the Morning:

Ms. Shuni, the other Media Center Professional, had just walked into the office area from one of the classrooms, where she had been consulting with a teacher. "Conichiwa," she said as she passed Isaac's desk. It was Japan week.

"Conichiwa, Margaret-san," Isaac replied, with a prayer bow gesture.

The 32-year library media specialist walked over to her desk, fit her tablet into its cradle, and touched the print login surface of her keyboard with her thumb, causing a virtual connection between the two devices through the room's wireless network. As she began typing an e-mail message, a group of students ambled into the media center. Mr. Johnson rose from his desk and strolled out into the larger room to see if he was needed.

Desmone, a member of Sally's Reptiles, said something to the group she was with and then walked over to Isaac. She was visibly anxious. "Mr. Johnson, Alf got in trouble again last night." Isaac motioned to a nearby unoccupied work area, and they both walked over and sat. "Have you heard from him? Have you seen him here at school yet? Will he be here for our presentation today?"

Isaac asked the girl for her tablet and then pressed the print login with his index finger so that the information appliance could reconfigure itself for his access. He then pulled up the school's information system and learned that Alf's nametag had not been registered for the day. "He isn't in the building yet," said Isaac.

Isaac then accessed the call-in register to see if Alf's mother had called indicating that he would not be in school that day. "His mother hasn't called in. Right now, it looks like he will be here." After a pause, Mr. Johnson said, "Just a minute!"

He pulled up the work folder for the Reptile's project and accessed Alf's video presentation, the part of the project in which he had been most engaged. Mr. Johnson touched the icon for the student's file, then touched the menu bar at the top of the display to select "Info" from the drop down list of options. A small white document appeared with statistical information on the file including its size, type, location, and other data. Mr. Johnson touched the word "history" and a second document sprang out. After reading the list of entries there, he looked up at Desmone, smiled, handed the tablet over after touching an icon to erase his configuration, and said, "I think Alf will be here today!"

As she reached for her tablet, Desmone noticed that her friends had gathered their things and were headed out of the room. She quickly thanked the educator, with some uncertainty, and turned to join her friends.

At the ring of the bell, Sally rises and walks over to the door, shaking the hand of each student as he or she enters the room. She smiles as she sees Alf walking rapidly down the hall to join the group as it enters her classroom. A tall young man with uncombed curly brown hair, the dark complexion of a boy who spends a lot of time outdoors, and the customary awkwardness of a teenager who is growing too fast, he shakes Ms. Crabtree's hand, but does not look up at her, moving away and toward his seat in the rear of the room.

As she turns to her classroom, she recalls the morning visit from Mr. Ball, the balding and portly principal.

Earlier in the Morning:

Ms. Crabtree looked up in mock irritation as the 31-year educator Mr. Ball spun one of the rolling student desks over to her work area and sat heavily in the seat without consideration of his greater than average size. Sally and Mr. Ball had been friends for all of the eight years that he has been the chief administrator of Bacon, both professionally and personally. Their long friendship and professional relationship did not require niceties. He began with the heart of the problem. "Alf Greeley was taken in by the police last night for vandalism," he said.

Sally sighed and replied, "It was probably another fight with his mother. He is still hurting so much from their split, and she simply does not know how her reaction is making things worse for her son."

"All we can do is to try and keep him engaged in his projects and help him in anyway that we can," Mr. Ball said. "I just thought you should know so that you can handle things accordingly."

"His team, the Reptiles, is making its ecology movement presentation today." Sally finally smiled at her friend and boss. "If you were to casually come in to watch, it would be an encouraging gesture."

Mr. Ball stood and said, "Send me a message when they are getting started, and I'll do what I can!"

As the principal shoved the abducted seat back in the direction of the other desks, Sally pulled up her e-mail utility, addressed a message to Mr. Ball, and wrote the note, "Reptiles are starting their presentation! -SC-". She set it for delayed delivery; it would be sent directly to his pocket tablet upon her click of a Send icon that suddenly appeared in a corner of her tablet.

Sally returns to her desk, picks up her tablet, and glances at the attendance document that automatically appears; it indicates that one of her B2 students is not present, but that he is on the campus. Attendance remains a political necessity, but teachers no longer have to call the roll since the campus proximity system knows the location of all students and faculty on campus by their nametag chips.

A series of checks by the student names also appears on her class roll, indicating that the students have submitted their class assignments. Some checks indicate initial submission of the work; other checks indicate that submitted work has been reviewed by the teacher, reworked by the student, and re-submitted. One student name has no check by it, but one suddenly appears as she is scanning the list. She looks up at the youngster who blushes and returns his attention to his tablet.

She touches with her finger the Send icon at the corner of her information appliance, and the short message, written earlier in the morning, is sent directly to Mr. Ball's pocket tablet.

As Sean, the missing student, walks quickly into the room, he shakes Ms. Crabtree's hand distractedly and finds his desk. Sally announces, "As you know, today the Reptiles ("slither, slither" the members murmur at the mention of their team name) will make their presentation. I have to say that I am very excited about this presentation. Johann, Desmone,

Alf, and Samuel have all worked very hard on their report, and I think you will learn a great deal from this presentation."

Ms. Crabtree continues, "But before we get started, I want to mention that you have an assignment posted on your calendars. I want you to read a short story written by a teenager from Croatia. A2 read it yesterday, and we had some very interesting discussions about the story today. Mr. Johnson also contacted the author and she sent a video file in which she explains why she wrote the story. You are welcome to access A2's discussion and Nadia Kaufman's video file from the school's video archive.

"Now, without any further ado, I introduce to you, the Reptiles."

With the team's customary "slither, slither" chant, the room darkens and the front display board goes black; Johann manipulates icons on his tablet with a glowing stylus. As the room turns dark, the classroom door opens and clicks shut as Mr. Ball walks quietly in and sits in a seat toward the back of the room. From the center of the room, Desmone speaks, "The Institute of Ecosystem Studies' definition of ecology is 'Ecology is the scientific study of the processes influencing the distribution and abundance of organisms, the interactions among organisms, and the interactions between organisms and the transformation and flux of energy and matter.'" White text of the definition gradually brightens into view on the large display with key terms shifting to red. Then the definition gradually fades away into black.

Desmone continues, "There are no guarantees. The world is in flux. Conditions change, and the ecological balance teeters here and there, sponsoring the loss of some species, and the introduction of new ones. Some weaken, and others become stronger..."

While she speaks, images of extinct species surface into view and then fade again; in the background and watermarked to about half brightness, two videos impose on each other. One displays a group of cheetahs chasing down a wildebeest that has been taken by surprise. The other shows a pride of lions failing to catch three gazelles that rapidly dart left and right out of reach. Desmone continues to speak and describes specific species of both animals and plants that have disappeared or changed dramatically, and the environmental conditions that seem to have caused the change.

Finally, the images fade to a map of the world done in negative relief, appearing as it did millions of years ago. A time line, beginning at about 200 million years ago, appears to the right of the map. A citation also appears in off-white, indicating a Web site that was the source of the data. Immediately, a pointer, starting at the bottom of the time line, starts to move up slowly. Simultaneously, landmasses begin to move in a motion with which the students are already familiar. Many of them have also used this animation from the Smithsonian Institute's Web site.

The team is not downgraded for using the familiar animation. However, the class becomes noticeably more interested as splotches begin to fade in and out in specific locations on the map. Numbers are imposed over the splotches as they gradually expand and become more opaque and then shrink to transparency. Soft but intense music plays in the background; it is credited to a talented student who had attended Bacon school two years earlier, and a short citation appears in the lower corner of the display. Samuel speaks over the animation and music and describes periods in the planet's relatively recent history of mass extinctions and seemingly spontaneous rises in species diversity.

"Each rise and fall has corresponded with some dramatic change in global conditions: ice ages, planetary collisions, volcanic or seismic calamities..." Samuel continues to speak eloquently.

As he continues, Ms. Crabtree is taken back to a conversation she had with the boy as the team worked on the ecology project. Samuel is thought by many to be a technical genius. He has a genuine gift for understanding and using technology. He also has a flair for using these tools to communicate persuasively. She had convinced Samuel, however, not to handle the programming and data manipulation for this project. She asked that he leave that up to Johann—that Samuel only be allowed to give Johann verbal directions. She had also asked Samuel to do more of the copy and script writing on this project, an activity that she knew would be a challenge for him.

Several Days Earlier:

Sally entered the school media center, a faint electronic click registering her entrance from the chip in her nametag. She stepped aside, so as not to block the doorway, and surveyed the room. The media center had far fewer books than it did when she went to middle school in the middle 1980s. There was a section in one corner that consisted of shelves with books of various sizes and colors. They were almost exclusively fiction books that students checked out for pleasure and for assignments in their humanities classes. These books remained because it was a deeply held belief that students appreciated the experience of reading a story without the benefit of electronic appliances. Regardless, most reading was done with tablet computers and smaller pocket text and audio players.

The biggest portion of the room was devoted to work areas that Isaac called "Knowledge Gardens." Most of these workspaces consisted of a table, with a 19-inch display, attached to a folding cradle that could swivel 360°. The display could be assigned to any tablet in its vicinity when the owner touched the print login pad. Scattered around the table were small but efficient keyboards, each of which could also be assigned to any tablet with the touch of its print login pad.

There were also two small stages with 4- × 8-foot display boards where teams could practice their presentations. She also saw a number of work areas that were much more casual, with homey lamps, beanbag chairs, low sofas, and assorted pillows. The media center was set up for knowledge construction, not just information accessing. Students came here to work, and mostly to work in small groups. It was rarely a quiet place.

Sally found the Reptiles and walked over. All four were together discussing their defense of one of the information resources they were using. She caught Samuel's eye and asked if he would join her for a minute. She had read through the talented young man's text document for the project; it was comprehensive and well organized. It appeared, though, that he had paid very little attention to grammar and sentence structure.

They sat down at an unoccupied table, and Sally laid her tablet down. "I wanted to talk for just a minute about your report," she said

"I'm not finished with it yet, Ms. Crabtree," Samuel immediately replied, somewhat defensively.

The defensive plea was ignored by the veteran middle-school teacher. She expected the reaction from the young man who was more comfortable writing computer code than prose. "I wanted to discuss something anyway. It is a good time in your process."

The youngster resigned himself as Sally reached over and touched her index finger to the print login on the table's 19-inch display. Immediately her tablet display was mirrored to the larger device. She pulled up a comments file that had been sent regarding a project from the previous year by another team. Sally continued by complimenting the boy on his thoroughness and the overall organization of the document, specifically pointing out the logical flow. Then she said, "I want you to read these comments from an architect, concerning the introduction of a project last year to design a school campus of the future."

As Samuel read, Sally followed, reading it again. The architect had first applauded the students on their insights and technical abilities, but then criticized them brutally on the quality of their writing. The architect explained, "Poor written communication conveys a lack of respect for an audience, the product being described, and a lack of respect for the writer. Poor communication puts a blemish on the entire message or product that is difficult or impossible to remove again."

Isaac had walked up and was reading over their shoulders, having planned this meeting with Ms. Crabtree. Isaac said, "Writing text for people to read is a lot like writing computer code. Computer code is text that is written for a computer. You write it to convince the machine to do what you want it to do. If the syntax of the code is wrong, then the computer does not perform as you intended."

He continued, "You write for people in order to affect them in some way, to inform them about a topic or event, or to cause them to behave in some way. If your syntax is wrong, then you can fail in what you want to accomplish."

Samuel cocked his head slightly, a personal gesture indicating he was considering what the adults had said. Then he reminded Ms. Crabtree that he had not cleaned up the text but admitted that he had never thought about grammar in that way. He said that he might get Mr. Johnson or Ms. Shuni to recommend some instructional software to improve his intuitive grammar skills.

Ms. Crabtree is drawn back to the presentation as Alf rises and walks to the front of the room. As he turns to face the audience, he nods to Desmone, who begins the multimedia presentation. Sally can tell from the expression on Desmone's face that Desmone is nervous about controlling the presentation since she has not yet seen it.

The large screen goes black again; in rising volume, music begins to play a very slow and eerie piece with cellos, wooden blocks, and low flutes. A citation surfaces into view at the bottom of the screen in white, crediting the music to Alf Greeley. Ms. Crabtree's eyebrow rises as she acknowledges a new talent for this young man.

As the citation fades away again, a map of the world returns with a time line to the right that covers a 3,000-year range. The time line pointer moves up the centuries and more splotches of red began to expand out becoming opaque, and then receding back into transparency. As the visuals proceed and the music fades back, Alf begins to speak, casually walking across the front of the room, identifying various periods of social turmoil and listing the number of people killed in violence as the labels and numbers impose themselves over the splotches.

As the time line marker enters the later part of the second millennium, Alf describes the Protestant Reformation, the Inquisition, the Fall of Imperialism, the American Civil Rights Movement, and the American War on Drugs. Alf finally says, "And the war on ..." He stops abruptly.

Surfacing on top of the world map, a video clip materializes and shows the beating of Rodney King in 1992. Other video examples of violence by the police or military surface, play, and fade out of view and, as this occurs, Alf finishes his sentence, "... daring! Daring to be different, daring to resist, daring to celebrate or to mourn. Daring to be yourself in a world where fitting in makes things run smoother but makes people run cold."

Then he stops and walks back to his seat. The room is silent; even Desmone remains motionless, until she smiles to herself and then turns and smiles at Alf. It was a powerful presentation, and there was also the provocation of Alf's video clips. There would be much discussion of this presentation from the community, and many opportunities for the team to defend its work.

Later, after lunch, Sally sits in her classroom office reviewing the Reptiles' presentation. Her classes are over and she has the afternoon to engage in planning and other professional activities: review student work, do research for her own presentations, meet with students and teams on their progress, and participate in online meetings with other professionals and collaborators. All class performances are recorded and available through the school's video archives. She has isolated the Reptiles' morning presentation into a separate file, which she is now annotating with comments.

Beneath the video is another document displaying the rubric that had been agreed upon by the team. In most objectives, each member of the team receives excellent marks. For Alf, the objective that calls for compelling communication is an "A" easily. She checks him at "Exceeded Expectations." It was a striking presentation and the quality of the video editing was exquisite. He had never demonstrated such skill before and, if she did not know that scores meant little to Alf, she might have suspected unethical use of copyrighted information. The presentation would provoke reactions from the community. Sally notices that the outside comments bin is already filling up. She will spend a sizable part of the afternoon screening the comments for the students.

After reviewing the evaluations of the rest of the class and assessing the additional materials including student reflections on their project, Ms. Crabtree writes her initial comments for the team's review and then writes her customary letters of thanks to the members. As she finishes her letters, Alf Greeley walks into the room.

"Alf, how are you?" The teacher asks with genuine interest.

"I'm fine, I guess" the moody boy replies. Then he adds, "Ms. Crabtree, about the violence in my video…"

The teacher knew that this was coming. There is a hard rule in all presentations, especially for those including images and video, that there be no violence demonstrated.

"You could have stopped the presentation right then, but didn't," Alf continues.

"The reason for the policy is to avoid the glorification of violence. You weren't glorifying violence. You were using it to very effectively make a point. Your examples were not that different from the examples of the lions and the cheetah, which were also violent."

Alf nods in understanding and then looks directly at Ms. Crabtree and says, "Thanks!" It is sincere!

Meanwhile, Isaac Johnson's workday has entered its more intense period as the large media center fills up with students and student teams working on their projects. All of the knowledge gardens are occupied by groups consulting with each other or working individually on specific components of their presentations. Many wear headphones as they consult with other team members or collaborators via teleconferencing or work with musical keyboards composing and editing background music or sound effects.

Mr. Johnson notices Desmone standing by the bookshelf, apparently waiting to talk with him. He commends the students he is sitting with on their work, excuses himself, and walks over to the waiting teenager.

"I was just curious, Mr. Johnson," she begins as he approaches. "How did you know that Alf would be here today?"

The young educator smiles at Desmone. "Do you remember when I checked Alf's work files?" She nods. "His last work was done on a computer whose owner was labeled as Sgt. Jonathan Frick. I know Sergeant Frick. He works the night shift for the police department. Evidently, Alf finished up his part of your project from the police station."

Desmone cocks her head, not understanding.

Mr. Johnson continues, "Do you think Alf would have been working on his project at the police station if he had not fully intended to be in class for the presentation today?"

Desmone smiles. "Oh!" She immediately locks eyes with a friend across the media center and looks back to the media coordinator. "Thanks, Mr. Johnson!"

"You're quite welcome!" Mr. Johnson bows slightly.

Assumptions About the Future

This future fiction was only one speculation among many possibilities that depend on a nearly endless number of variables. I hope that you enjoyed it and, if you have any questions or comments about the story or the educational environment that framed it, please visit this book's online discussion boards at <http://landmark-project.com/redefining_literacy>.

Writing the story was a unique and an enlightening experience in itself. Speculating on the technologies that will likely be available in 10 years and then super-imposing a teaching and learning environment around those technologies caused me to reconsider a variety of issues related to education in a way that I had not in many years. As a result, many of my philosophical opinions about education at the beginning of the twenty-first century have been affected. This is good. As uncertain as it is, it is absolutely essential that a consideration of the future be part of every discussion we have and decision we make regarding what and how we teach. It is essential, in this time of rapid change, that we add futurist to the job description of teachers and facilitate ongoing research, discussion, and reflection about the future for which we are preparing our children.

At the same time that we consider the future, we should also be thinking about the technologies that will shape the learning environments that we will craft for our students. If you feel any sense of confidence in your mastery of the technologies of teaching and learning, I suggest you think about the following advancements.

Consider quantum computers, a brand new technology that is currently being researched and developed with some early success. The basis of quantum computing is its reliance on the behavior of quantum particles (electrons, protons, and particles even more fundamental and strange) to add, subtract, and remember things—the essence of computing. The benefit of quantum computing is that these machines would be able to operate at unimaginable speeds. I use the word *unimaginable* because at the quantum level, time does not exist. Therefore, many computations could be performed simultaneously, from a Newtonian perspective.

To stir things up even more, scientists in California, Canada, and Denmark are beginning to perform the first experiments in teleportation, causing an object in one location to suddenly appear in another (Shachtman <http://www.wired.com/news/technology/ 0,1282,47191,00.html>). Scientists are even succeeding in creating matter by forcing sub-atomic particles to shape themselves into specific atoms and molecules called designer matter (McCarthy <http://www.wired.com/wired/archive/9.10/atoms_pr.html>). You may one day stand in front of a machine and say, "Earl Grey—Hot." Suddenly, a quantity of vaporous gas turns itself into a piping hot drink served in an English tea service.

Now ask yourself, "How incredible does this sound, computers operating where time and space do not exist and the idea of Scottie beaming us around town?"

Hold that thought for just a moment.

Go back 10 years. It is 1994. The World Wide Web is in its infancy with only a handful of Web pages. Most of us have not even heard of the Internet. The author of this book, that you will one day read, steps into your classroom and suggests that, 10 years from now, the classroom you teach in will likely have at least one, and probably more, multimedia computer that is more powerful than the largest mainframes of 1990—and that each of these computers will be connected to a global electronic library of billions of pages of text, pictures, graphs, sounds, animations, and even video. Then ask yourself if this suggestion in 1994 would have seemed any less incredible then than my current description of machines that work outside the limits of time and space seems now.

Large Idea!

The process of preparing our children for their future should involve holding their hands and personally guiding them into their future.

We live in a time when only 10 years can see literally unimaginable changes in the tools that we use to accomplish our goals. At the same time, the basic fabric of our society changes much less quickly and with a greater deal of resistance—and this is fortunate. As an educator of more than 25 years, I must confess to what many might think is a romantic notion of education: that it should be based on a personal relationship between a teacher and his or her students, and that we should resist the temptation to rely too much on computers to do our teaching. The process of preparing our children for their future should involve holding their hands and personally guiding them into their future.

Teaching and learning through distance, using online tools and resources, are important parts of the education landscape. Distance learning solves important problems as we cope with the challenges of making a living in a rapidly changing and widening world. Michael Cox, the Chief Economist of the Federal Reserve Bank of Dallas, Texas, recently said to a group of students that they would "... have at least five jobs after (they) graduate, four of which have not been invented yet" (Mokhoff <http://www.eetimes.com/story/OEG20001031S0022>). If he is correct, and I suspect that he is, then being able to learn from any place and at any time will be part of prospering as an adult. Children, on the other hand, should prepare for their future within personal, face-to-face relationships. Socialization is an act of sharing, guiding, and nurturing. But the relationship is not one of teachers delivering instruction, with students passively receiving and storing that instruction. If our children's prosperity will be based on lifelong learning experiences, then perhaps the best thing we can teach them now is how to teach themselves.

Assumptions—New Tools

The story that you read was based on several assumptions about the future. Some of the assumptions are fairly certain. Others will depend on some rather slippery conditions that rely on changes in societal thinking. Yet they are not outside the realm of possibilities.

The technologies described in the story are probably the most certain assumptions. Computers have changed dramatically since the Radio Shack *Model I* computers that were in my classroom in 1981 and the Apple IIs and PCs that were available only 10 years ago. They are becoming increasingly powerful and mobile. Today, we are beginning to see laptop classrooms, where each student has access to a fast multimedia computer, connected wirelessly to the global Internet. In many schools, students are carrying around palm-sized machines of astonishing computing power.

If we are to teach our students to teach themselves, then we must make available for students the tools and information that will facilitate these skills. Students (and teachers) must have ubiquitous access to computers and net-worked information. At the point that a student (or teacher) has a question, he or she should have immediate access to relevant resources without the need to funnel the need through a teacher who is shared by 30 students, or a five-year-old and static textbook.

I suspect, though, that cumbersome laptop computers, with so much space devoted to the keyboard, will not make the best tool. Even though the keyboard will be with us for many years, it is probably not the most efficient means of input for the classroom. Handwriting is even more inefficient and labor intensive. Voice command, audio recording, and text transcriptions make much more sense, although these too have disadvantages.

Size is another consideration. If the palm of my hand was the most effective size for delivering instruction, then our textbooks would have the same dimensions of index cards today. Apple Computer introduced the first commercial Personal Digital Assistant (PDA), the Newton. It was about 50% larger than today's Palm machines, and it continues to be used, despite Apple's discontinuance of the product in 1998. The Newton is still supported by an online community of devoted programmers and enthusiasts who believe that its size and functionality are superior to today's Palm machines and hand-held PCs.

The Palm Pilot enjoyed sudden and enormous success because it did a very good job of performing only a few essential tasks: schedule, address book, and memos. The past few years have seen attempts to push this pocket-sized device to do things that, because of its size, it is not suited to do. Within 10 years, we will see a convergence of the laptop sized (tablet-sized) computer and the instant availability and flexibility of the flat touch-based hand-held computer.

Tablet PCs are enjoying a resurrection as I write this—not their first. Their focus continues to be note taking—handwriting recognition. Although this is an important capa-bility, I suspect that we are currently asking students to spend too much of their valuable instructional time writing things down, when they should be spending time in higher-order activities. I want to be able to lay my computer down and have it record the spoken words of a meeting or classroom, and then accurately transcribe the words into text, assigning statements to the speakers. I would be free to listen, consider, interact, and contemplate. I would later have access to the information by searching the transcript for keywords and phrases.

Another assumption related to the technology we will be using is that information becomes more valuable when it is delivered in the most efficient format or formats. As highly as we regard reading, most of us spend an enormous amount of time watching video

Large Idea!

... perhaps the best thing we can teach our children now is how to teach themselves.

in the form of TV programming, commercials, or movies. We also view images and animations and listen to information being spoken to us. Well-produced video is compelling, as are carefully rendered images, graphs, and animation. We should be able to utilize these media formats much more freely and frequently and the required technology should be an integral part of every classroom. The tools to communicate effectively with students should not have to be *checked-out* from the media center.

In 2000, I had an opportunity to visit a number of schools in Hong Kong. The classrooms in these schools all had multimedia projectors mounted on the ceilings; the projectors were connected to powerful desktop computers at the teachers' desks. Teachers were able to display a wide range of information using the media format most appropriate to the instructional goal and the information styles of the students. Interactive media is replacing the chalkboard. Interactive display boards are rapidly appearing in our schools, and I suspect that plasma-type flat displays will be next, possibly in the next five years. In fact, there are a number of companies that are currently marketing E-Paper, nearly paper-thin material that serves as a computer display, which is able to reprint itself based on instructions from a computer. E-paper can be rolled up or pasted to any flat surface. Consider electronic wallpaper in your classroom where you could display content on any wall or other flat surface—cheaply.

Finally, in this school (and community) of 2014, the information will be in the air. Wireless access to content will be almost ubiquitous. It has already begun. Large parts of this book were written in coffee houses, airports, and hotel lobbies where the Internet is freely accessed with a wireless-equipped notebook computer. This increasing access to a world of knowledge begs the question, "What will our libraries become, when all knowledge is available through personal information devices—anytime, anyplace?"

Hold that thought.

Assumptions—What We Do with New Tools

The following assumptions will be more difficult to achieve than producing and even procuring new technologies. They apply less to the appearance of the classroom and more to our practice of teaching and learning. They depend less on the market-driven advance of technology, and more on people's willingness to invest in fundamental changes in schools and schooling.

As I conduct staff development with teachers across the United States and discuss the barriers that prevent teachers from retooling their teaching, the number one barrier that arises is a lack of time. The fact is that most teachers today have less time on the job to prepare their lessons, plan, evaluate, collaborate, develop materials, research, and gain new skills than my teachers had in the 1950s and '60s. This severe shortage of time persists even though we are preparing our students for a far more dynamic future within a more rapidly changing and demanding present.

Many teachers do spend a great deal of time preparing lessons, planning, evaluating, collaborating, developing materials, researching, and gaining new skills. However, they do it on their own time, at the expense of their families, their health, and too often, at the expense of our students, as more and more teachers are leaving the profession every month. I suspect that this exodus has less to do with salaries than it does with the condition of the job and the personal cost of succeeding as a teacher.

Because of the challenges of preparing today's children for a largely unknown future, it is time to stop forcing teachers to work harder, and start helping them to work smarter, giving them the time to create and craft relevant learning environments and experiences for their students. This is the best thing that we could do to help retool classrooms for the twenty-first century. The one constant that appears in almost all education research is that the key to good learning is a good teacher, and there are many mediocre teachers who could become great teachers with more time for planning.

I have already confessed my romantic notions that education should be based on a face-to-face relationship between teacher and student. Still, we will discover over the next few years, there are some things that students learn better in a traditional classroom setting, and that they learn other things best while sitting at a computer, operating software, conducting research, collaborating with other students or experts, and building personally meaningful information products. Being engaged in these activities depends less on where the student is, and more on the quality of the assignment. We may find that students only need to be in traditional classrooms for four hours a day, and teachers can attend to the other professional activities involved in teaching during their remaining time on the job. Students would engage in their information explorations and constructions in school centers, commercial and public learning support facilities, day care sites, and partly at home; and they would be supervised by education-savvy information, research, and production experts.

I suspect that as we move toward personal information devices, our *tablets*, and away from 20- and 30-pound book bags, there will be an increasing market for dynamic digital textbooks that our students will use anywhere, any time. At the same time, as teachers and students become more accustomed to the volumes of information that are available on the Internet and the extreme flexibility of digital information, we could easily see a different shift regarding textbooks. Traditionally, students have been viewed exclusively as consumers of information, mostly from their textbooks. In the future, students may be viewed more as constructors of knowledge and producers of information. Students, rather than consuming their textbooks, will produce their own textbook. It was once popular to have students keep notebooks for their courses, which teachers would check every grading period for accuracy and completeness. This model could easily be extended to the computer where students would be required to assemble their own digital textbooks with content that they collect from the Internet and other sources in formats that make the most sense to them, and then use their personal digital textbooks as growing references for their continued study. Teachers would digitally supervise the construction of these personal textbooks via the network, to assure that the students' references are accurate, appropriate, and useful.

Large Idea!

... stop forcing teachers to work harder, and start helping them to work smarter ...

Assumptions—Curriculum and the New Tools

Imagine a typical Information Age workplace. As you look around, you are probably standing inside a cubical with Dilbert cartoons taped on the wall. We will not disturb the cartoons, but as you look down you see a telephone lying on the desk and plugged into the wall. As you consider this phone, chances are great that you have a cell phone in your pocket, attached to your belt, or lying in your purse. In fact, you may have already dropped your landline at home because you found it to be redundant to the cell phones that the members of your family carry with them. As I suggest this in workshops and conference presentations, teachers are increasingly raising their hands, indicating that they have disconnected and discontinued their traditional telephone service and rely exclusively on mobiles. With this trend in mind, I will simply remove the telephone from our Information Age workplace. It is clear that communication in our students' future will involve personal technologies that students carry with them.

We continue to look around and see a number of bins, each labeled and holding stacks of paper. There are also a number of bound reports stacked on a shelf hanging from one of the walls. As we examine these papers and reports, consider that according to a study conducted by the School of Information Management and Systems of the University of California at Berkeley, we will generate five exabytes of new information this year. That equates to about 800 megabytes of information for every man, woman, and child on the planet. The kicker is that only .01% (that is one one-hundredth of one percent) of that information is ever printed (Regents of the University of California <http://www.sims.berkeley.edu/how-much-info/summary.html>). The remainder of the information is machine-readable. If the information that we are generating today is almost exclusively digital, then we will remove the papers and bound reports from our cubicle, assuming that information in the future will reside in cyberspace.

While we're at it, we will remove the books as well. No more books! Now the irony of suggesting a demise of books, while you read this book, does not escape me. Again, I am a romantic, and I believe that this world would be a sadder place without books. However, I also understand that the future of books is not in our hands, but in the hands of our children and their children, and indications are that future generations will prefer to have information that is digital, abundant, and able to fit into their pockets. I can only guarantee that we will continue to have books for one more generation. After that, I do not know!

In 2000, Microsoft predicted that by 2018, when we speak or hear the word "book," we will automatically think of an electronic form of the medium. If we mean the traditional paperbound variety, we will have to say, "paper book" (Microsoft 1999). Granted, this is the same Microsoft that said that "640 K would be enough (computer memory) for anyone." Still we have to take into account that we are not purchasing encyclopedias and many other information products in the same way that we did 10 years ago. We are purchasing them as digital products, because we have found that the information has more value when it is digital than it does on paper. So the paper has disappeared from our future Information Age workplace.

I was recently invited to tour the Media Lab at MIT. If you have not heard of the Media Lab, Stewart Brand called it the place where they are "… inventing the future" in his book *The Media Lab*. As I was led around this building, designed by the architect, I.M. Pei, I was struck by its presence. The sole purpose of this building was to invent, using tools and concepts about which most people have never heard. The items that almost immediately caught my attention were the tiny video cameras that I saw, mounted on pencil-thin support rods, stationed at nearly every work area. They stood on every desk, coffee table, and work surface; every place where people might work included one of these quarter-sized cameras. I also noticed that nearly every lab and office held a large multimedia display. Often there were projectors mounted on the ceiling, but in many cases there were plasma-style flat panels hanging on the wall.

When I asked about the cameras, I was told that there was a very good reason for their presence. For these researchers, collaboration is everything. They pay a great deal of attention to what their colleagues are studying, and when someone finds that a fellow scientist is working in an area that may impact his or her work, then the two will want to collaborate. However, scheduling time, place, and supporting technologies and infrastructure for collaborative meetings is not a productive use of time. So the scientists simply configure the cameras and displays in their work areas so that they can see and hear each other from their own respective workplaces. The effect is to produce a virtual doorway between the two work areas, giving the scientists a sense of being together in the same place. It does not matter if one scientist is on the first floor and the other is on the third, or if one is at Media Lab in Cambridge and the other is with a European counterpart in Dublin, Ireland. They have connected their offices so that they can work in collaboration.

This is actually not such a dramatic feat when you can go out today, purchase a small video camera for less than $100, plug it into the USB port of your computer, install some software, and carry on videoconferences with friends, family, and professional colleagues over the Internet. Considering that we may increasingly hold our meetings online in the future, we will take out the extra chairs in our cubicles.

Scanning around further, we find a desktop computer sitting in a corner with a slide-out keyboard and mouse stand. Yet, today, we could easily replace that machine with a sleek laptop that has nearly the screen size and computing power, and the added benefit of being able to take it with you. Futurists predict that we will soon be wearing our technology. This has already begun as many of us carry small computers and communication devices in our pockets or wear them on our belts. However, we may soon be wearing technology as jewelry, in our eyeglasses, or stitched into our clothing. These devices will constantly be in contact with each other, sharing pertinent information, and talking not only with the devices on our persons, but also with other appliances, telling us when the milk is going bad in the refrigerator or how to cook the meal that we just put in the microwave, or informing us that the alternator in our car needs to be replaced, letting us know the service centers in the area that have the part in stock.

Now I am not saying that I personally approve of these suggested advances. I prefer that my technology be something I can leave behind without removing my clothing. Nevertheless, computers will not be something that must be left on the desk, nor will it even require a desk to operate. So at the same time that we remove the computer, we will take out the desk as well, since there is nothing left on it.

What do we have left in our Information Age work area? Almost nothing.

Large Idea!

For the first time in history, our job, as educators, is to prepare our students for a future that we cannot clearly describe.

And this is exactly what we know about the future for which we are preparing our students—*Almost Nothing*.

For the first time in history, our job, as educators, is to prepare our students for a future that we cannot clearly describe. We have always known, with certainty, what our children would be doing 10 years from now, or 20, or even 30 years. Today, the future we are preparing our students for is impossible to describe. Things are changing too quickly. We can only predict that it will be a world driven by information, and that the information will be almost exclusively digital.

Again, I do not necessarily approve of the suggestions I have made in this activity, and some were made with a certain amount of tongue-in-cheek. Nevertheless, it is undeniable that our children will be challenged to succeed, prosper, and find personal fulfillment in an environment that to us will seem strange and confusing. If we do our jobs right, it will be an intensely exciting time for our children.

Critical Questions for Educators

There are four critical questions that education, as a democratic force, must continually ask. They are:

- **Who will we teach?**
- **What will we teach them?**
- **How will we teach them?**
- **How well are we succeeding?**

Who will be taught is a question that we struggled with during the last years of the twentieth century. When I attended school in the 1950s and '60s, there were children who simply slipped out of our classrooms and into obscurity with almost no notice. Many were less than the required age for compulsory education: 16. However, little or no effort was exerted to find and return these children to the classroom. The fact of the matter was that there were plenty of jobs, in the mills of my hometown, for which these children were sufficiently qualified. Today, children remain in our classrooms because we have decided that the answer to the **Who** question is, "Everyone."

The question that we seem most concerned with today is the **How Well**. Measuring learning and holding schools accountable for their students' learning appears to be the prevailing formula for education reform. States are now mandated to develop standardized tests to assess student learning in reading and math, and ultimately in other subject areas. **How well** is not a bad question, but it is a premature question. Under *No Child Left Behind* legislation, **How** is also being addressed to some degree by emphasizing practices based on scientific research. Creating a central clearinghouse of proven teaching strategies is also not a bad idea, as long as we do not forget that teaching is not exclusively a scientific and technical endeavor. It is based more on a social and personal relationship between teacher, student, and content. We must insist on retaining the teacher-philosopher in our efforts to produce teacher-technicians.

On the other hand, we hear very little about the **What** question in discussions of education reform. We talk about higher standards, but little is being done to rethink what children need to be learning in a time of rapid change. It is time that we reverse the priority of the questions we, as educators, consider asking first: what do students need to know for an unpredictable future, then how should they learn these skills and content, and finally figure out how to assure that we are succeeding (See figure 1.1).

Priority of Education Questions

Current Priority		Appropriate Priority

Current Priority

1. How well are students learning?
2. How should students learn?
3. What should students learn?

Reverse Order

Appropriate Priority

1. What should students learn?
2. How should students learn?
3. How well are students learning?

Figure 1.1: Educational Priorities

The challenge of this book is primarily to explore **What** students should be learning. If successful, the **How** and **How Well** will follow as a matter of course, building themselves out of the context of a new literacy and the changing environment that demands it. In other words, what is literacy in the twenty-first century, and how do we teach it to our children?

The purpose of this book is to expand our notions of what it means to be literate in the twenty-first century. This book does not define additional information literacy, or digital literacy, but a redefinition of basic literacy, what we might call **Contemporary Literacy** (Friesen page 1). It reaffirms the essence and vital importance of reading, writing, and basic mathematics but refines them within the context of an information environment that is: digital, global, indexed, hyper-organized, multimedia, ubiquitous; and a future political, economic, and personal experience that is largely driven by that information. When I was in school, we talked of the 3Rs as a way of describing the basic skills of the time. Today, we should talk about the 3Es (See figure 1.2).

	Twentieth Century Literacy	Twenty-first Century Contemporary Literacy
Expose the Information	Reading what someone has handed to you	Exposing meaning from a global, an interactive, and a multimedia electronic cybrary
Employ Information	Basic skills in mathematics	Mathematics and computer skills applied to solving information challenges and constructing information products from digital information
Express Ideas Compellingly	Writing	Digitally expressing ideas fluently and compellingly through text, image, animation, sound, and video to a broad and geographically diverse audience

Figure 1.2: The Three Es

It is also absolutely essential that these powerful skills be taught within a growing context for students that includes who they are and how their natural, cultural, social, and ethical environment influences them; and how they influence that environment.

Gail Morse, one of the original Christa McAuliffe educators, says that we were "paper-trained" in our classrooms—taught to use paper. Our students must be "light-trained."

Bring on the light!

2 Exposing the Information

For Christmas, 2000, I received a book that my uncle had written. The book was entitled *What I Know About My Ancestors*. It was not a long book, because there is not that much to tell. However, it was fascinating to read through the stories he had gleaned from his research and family legends going back to Johann Daniel Warlick's arrival in America in the early 18th century.

As I read the book, following the generations through the decades, one impression persisted. Being familiar with the geographic area in which the family settled, in the western piedmont of North Carolina, I envisioned their rural homes. Many miles from the nearest town, it is unlikely that they had access to books, pamphlets, or newspapers. There was very little media in their lives. In contrast, back through my grandfather's generation, education was considered very important to the family. Young men were sent to a boarding school in Pennsylvania for high school. My grandfather and one of his brothers earned college degrees, one in engineering at North Carolina State University, and the other in the Classics at the University of North Carolina. But regardless of this unusually high regard for education, they still had little information available to them on a daily basis.

What did education mean then and there? What did it mean to be educated in a time and place where recorded information was scarce? Education assured that knowledge was learned and remembered. Being educated meant that you held a great deal of information in your memory, and that you gained that knowledge largely through reading, listening, and reciting within a formal and regimented educational setting.

Today, we find ourselves in an environment that is radically different and dominated by information. The very physical environment that we live in is largely defined by information, and we interact with that environment using information. In addition, an increasing amount of that environment-defining information is online, and this trend will certainly continue.

Consider a journey I might take to Boston to attend a conference. If I were to drive the trip, I would likely go to a Web site to plot my course, receiving practical turn-by-turn instructions taking me from my home in North Raleigh to the door of the convention center. If I decide to spend the night in Pennsylvania, and I collect Priority Points from Holiday Inn, I would visit its Web site for a list of hotels, with amenities and prices, on my route. I might then reserve the room online and receive a map with the hotel's location. If I have a preference for the southern cooking of Cracker Barrel, I could visit its site to pinpoint its locations and plan my meal times. There may even be state Department of Transportation Web sites that identify problem areas of road construction and high congestion times and offer real-time video from Web cams along the way. To top it off, I could shop for a good mystery book, purchase it, and download the book from the Internet as an MP3 file to listen to during my travel. Now this experience is far from perfect yet. For instance, my route plotting service of choice sends me through downtown Washington, D.C., rather than taking me around the city on the beltway. In addition, this kind of planning takes away from the sheer adventure of making a long trip into unfamiliar territory.

In July 2003, I drove across North Carolina and Virginia, delivering a number of workshops to schools and districts in both states. For the trip, I rented a car with a global positioning system (GPS) installed on the dash. I simply typed in the town to which I was driving, selected the hotel where I was registered, and the GPS plotted my route, based on my choice to drive major highways, or the back roads. Each time I approached a turn, the device spoke to me, giving me details about the upcoming road changes. Once, I missed a turn in a particularly complicated cloverleaf, finding myself on the wrong Interstate highway traveling 70 miles an hour in the wrong direction. The GPS quickly re-plotted my route based on my current location. No problem. At any point along the way, I could receive a list of the next five exits, complete with information on the restaurants, service stations, and hotels available at each. Twice I picked up my cell phone, called directory assistance, and was connected to my favorite pizza restaurant in the town I was approaching. I ordered my mushroom and pepper pie over the phone, asked for the address, entered it into the GPS, and 20 minutes later was sitting down to a steaming delight. It was all defined by information; information that would not have been available in such a dynamic and useful way only 10 years ago.

This vast amount of networked information will not be exclusively intended for human consumption. Perhaps the next refrigerator that you purchase will be able to detect the expiration date of your milk and remind you to replace it. Merloni Elettrodomestici, a maker of home appliances in Italy, currently produces a refrigerator that will display messages on a front panel, such as, "Eat the yogurt on the bottom shelf within one day." The next generation will order more yogurt from the store and have it delivered to its home based on a schedule, which it will access from the handheld computer in someone's pocket.

The refrigerator will tell you all of this the next time you open its door, or perhaps it will even call you on your mobile phone.

The point is that information will be vast, diverse, and immediately available to the knowledgeable information consumer, and it will be digital. There is a significant difference between the quantity and quality of information today and the information world of my ancestors. Much of this change has occurred since I attended school in the 1950s and '60s, long before personal computers, CD-ROMs, the Internet, and mobile telephones.

When I was taught to read, I was taught to read what someone handed to me. I was taught to read the textbook provided by the teacher, and the reference books to which my school librarian guided me. I was taught to read the newspapers and magazines that were provided by publishers. If I could read and understand the text that someone gave to me, then I was considered literate.

In the twenty-first century, literacy involves not just reading and comprehending the text in front of you, but a wide range of skills associated with acquiring, decoding, evaluating, and organizing information within a global electronic library. Almost all of the information that our students use in their future will be viewed with a personal information device (a computer), and it will come from a global electronic library that will be vast, largely unman-

Large Idea!

In the twenty-first century, literacy involves ... a wide range of skills associated with acquiring, decoding, evaluating, and organizing information within a global electronic library.

aged, and produced from a bewildering variety of perspectives. If all our children learn to do is read, they will not be literate.

A Brief History of Networked Digital Information

The Internet, in its earliest beginnings, happened after I graduated from college and started teaching Social Studies. Although I started using modems and e-mail in 1984, I did not even hear about the Internet until six years later in 1990. At that time, I probably knew, by name, most of the K–12 educators who were on the Internet. In 1990, if you wanted to access information from this "network of networks," you had to use a program called FTP—an abbreviation for File Transfer Protocol. This was essentially DOS for the Internet, a series of cryptic commands that you typed into the computer to list, move, or copy files from one computer's hard drive to another computer's drive. The exhilaration came from the fact that these computers could be thousands of miles apart from each other. We were wizards with the secret incantations to transport information around the world.

The Internet first became popular among people outside of the tech world with the advent of Gopher, which was invented at the University of Minnesota. This new method for accessing information from the Internet arranged the known files into an almost endless cascade of menus. You would access your favorite Gopher site and receive a numbered menu of general subjects. Typing the number of the subject that most closely applied to your problem would reveal a new menu of topics, all related to the subject that you selected. Then you would type the number of the most relevant topic and receive another list of subtopics. Finally, after browsing through this branching tree of menus, you would receive a list of files, all related in some way to the final subtopic that you selected.

The important achievement of Gopher was that, for the first time, we were using information as the steering wheel for navigating the Information Highway. We moved around, seeking out the answers to our questions from a logical, information-based perspective, rather than typing cryptic incantations into the machine.

It was not long after Gopher appeared that a team of researchers, principally Tim Berners-Lee, at the Particle Physics Lab (CERN) in Geneva, Switzerland, invented the World Wide Web (WWW). Primarily, this new system enabled authors to link specific words and phrases within a computer file to other related files. Readers could select, using their **Tab** and **Enter** keys, the word or phrase they wanted to explore more deeply and automatically receive the related file—from someplace out on the Internet. No longer was the information inside the library, but the library was inside the information. This had staggering implications in the information community, but no one could have predicted the impact it would have in only 10 years. Even though the WWW was originally designed for a very specific group of physicists, the Internet was a small place in 1992, and news traveled fast.

Still, WWW did not truly catch on until an undergraduate student at the University of Illinois wrote a program called Mosaic and made it available on the Internet for free. This innovative new software enabled Web document authors to embed not only links, but also images in their pages, and readers of the pages could use their mouses to point and click the links. This was the *Killer App* (killer application) that launched the World Wide Web and Internet into our businesses, schools, and homes. Mosaic eventually became Netscape; Microsoft eventually saw the light and made Internet Explorer; and the rest is history—or the future.

This fieldtrip through the evolution of networked information is important to us as educators because it has largely happened since the birth of my children, neither of whom has reached college age yet. The nature of information, as they understand it, is dramatically different from how it looked and behaved when most of us were students. It surrounds them almost constantly. My children enjoy access to the global electronic library from their bedrooms, but before they graduate from college, they will probably carry access in their pockets or under their arms. They are not limited to their textbooks and the material available in their school library. We as educators have lost control over the information. Children control it now. They need to learn to control their information in positive, productive, and personally meaningful ways—and this is what we need to be teaching them.

Before we begin exploring strategies for finding information on the Internet, it is important to take just one more look at the nature of Net-based information. You and I were taught to read in two dimensions—across and down. Our students are accustomed to reading in a third dimension: across, down, and deeper into the information (See figure 2.1). By clicking through words, phrases, and images, they are able to dig into the information, moving deeper into greater understanding. This 3-D arrangement adds value to the message you are trying to deliver in that it points to supporting documents, and related documents can point to yours.

Students should understand this concept both as a way of navigation and also as a way to add value to their own information products. It is not necessary to teach students to use sophisticated Web editing programs in order to teach them to produce hyper-documents. Many of the popular word processing programs, including Microsoft Word and Appleworks, have hypertext features (See figure 2.2).

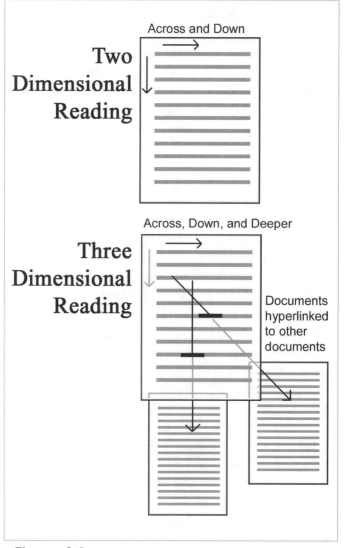

Figure 2.1: Three-Dimensional Reading

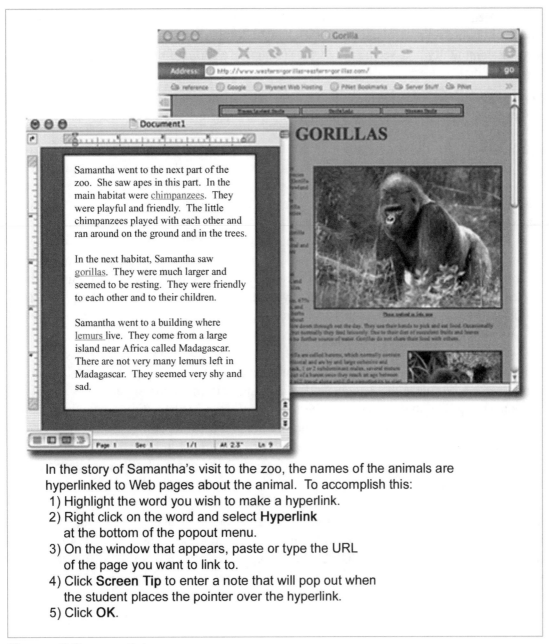

In the story of Samantha's visit to the zoo, the names of the animals are hyperlinked to Web pages about the animal. To accomplish this:
1) Highlight the word you wish to make a hyperlink.
2) Right click on the word and select **Hyperlink** at the bottom of the popout menu.
3) On the window that appears, paste or type the URL of the page you want to link to.
4) Click **Screen Tip** to enter a note that will pop out when the student places the pointer over the hyperlink.
5) Click **OK**.

Figure 2.2: Hyperlinks

As an example, your third-grade class might be asked to read a story about Samantha's visit to the zoo. You have typed the story into a word processor so that as the students read at their computers, they have access to the word processor's features. You might ask the students to browse through one of the kid-friendly Web directories or search engines (Yahooligans <http://www.yahooligans.com> or KidsClick <http://sunsite.berkeley.edu/KidsClick!/>) and select a Web page that corresponds with each of the animals they read about. Then students can turn the story into a hypertext document by converting the names of the animals in the story into hyperlinks that connect to the animals' Web pages. Depth can be added to the assignment by asking students to learn one thing about each animal from the Web page that they link to, and add what they learn to the text of the story.

Students could then save their hypertext stories on disk, share them with classmates, or take them home for their parents. The students' files can also be saved as Web pages and posted for community use, seeing how your students are adding to the World Wide Web.

Investigative Strategies— Personal Information Digital Libraries

The first strategy for finding information on the Internet is not really a search strategy. You probably have a personal library of professional books from college courses or graduate school, or books that you have purchased at workshops and conferences. You keep these books together and organized in one place because they consistently have information that helps you do your job.

Keeping a personal digital information library is just as important and for exactly the same reason. You probably keep bookmarks or favorites on your computer, and you may organize them into folders and sub-folders based on what you typically do when using the Web. You may organize them by the subjects you teach or your class periods. You may also have sub-folders for various units that you teach. You keep these bookmarks because they link to Web sites that consistently have information that helps you do your job.

The concept of the personal digital information library is one of the most compelling ideas that came out of writing the future fiction story at the beginning of this book. The Internet is a big place that is constantly changing both in its content and how we go about connecting with that content. Teachers, especially, do not have time to conduct deep research every time they seek out information to prepare the next unit of instruction. However, if they can easily keep and cultivate a personal digital information library and organize it in ways that are personally and professionally meaningful, these online libraries become a very effective first place to look for information that helps teachers teach.

Your bookmarks or favorites are a good place to start. The key to keeping bookmarks that are truly useful is organization. It is easy to do and adds value to your information, and you tend to take advantage of the information more frequently. I will not provide specific instructions here for organizing your bookmarks. Instructions vary between PC and Macintosh and across the versions of Netscape Navigator, Microsoft Internet Explorer, and the many other browsers. If you cannot figure it out, offer your tech facilitator some cookies and ask her to show you. For the most part, it is a matter of dragging a Web link into the proper bookmark folder.

In figure 2.3, folders have been created for the teacher's two subjects: World Civilizations and U.S. History. The U.S. History folder is open, revealing sub-folders for three units: Exploration, Colonial, and Revolution. The Colonial folder is open so that as she researches the Internet for appropriate Web sites, all she has to do is grab the link to "The 13 Colonies of America" Web site and drag it into the folder. It is a simple task and the resource is available to the teacher from this point on within the context of what and how she teaches.

One of the problems of using a browser's bookmarks comes from the fact that teachers typically use a number of computers in their work: computers in the classroom, computer lab, teachers' lounge, media center, and at home. Under most conditions, these bookmarks cannot be carried from one computer to another. This problem has been solved to some degree by a number of Web-based bookmark services, first introduced to educators by the education technology visionary John Kuglin when he delivered the keynote address at

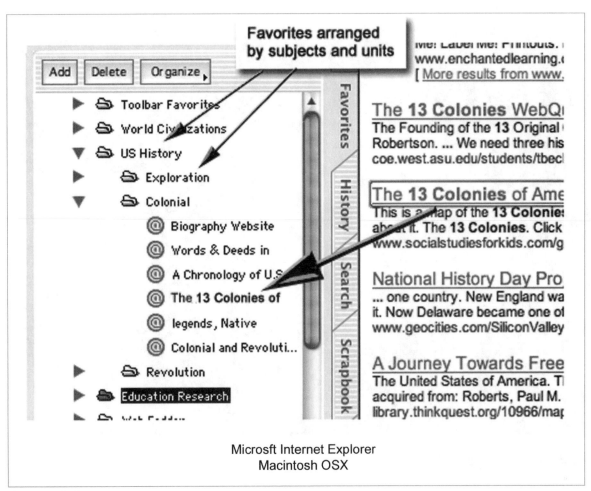

Figure 2.3: Bookmarks

the National Educational Computing Conference in 2000. He brought the house down as he demonstrated **Backflip** (<http://www.backflip.com>).

Like similar services, Backflip enables Internet users to create folders of topics that interest them and then save Web pages as bookmarks within the folders. It is just as practical as your bookmarks and has the added benefit that you can access the service from any computer on the Internet. Being digital means having it anywhere, anytime.

The Landmark Project has constructed a similar tool specifically for teachers called **PiNet Library** (<http://pinetlibrary.com>), short for Personal Internet Library. It works in the same way as Backflip, but also offers a number of services specifically for educators. Perhaps one of the most important features is the fact that teachers can share their folders, or Web *Shelves*, with other teachers so that Web resources that are added by any educator sharing a shelf are available to all members. For instruction, PiNet can also be used to easily and quickly create interactive WebQuest-style activities for students utilizing Web links from your library. Teachers and other educators can also create Web sites using PiNet Library and publish formatted lists of links directly from their Web shelves.

There are other ways to turn your computer into a personal digital information library. I run a program on my Macintosh called Drop Drawers from **Sig Software** (<http://www.sigsoftware.com/dropdrawers>). The product places three tabs on the edge of

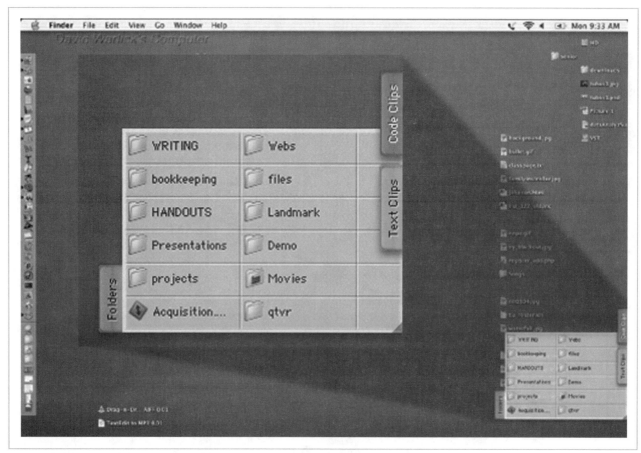

Figure 2.4: Drop Drawers

my screen that, when clicked, slide out drawers with links to files and folders on my hard drive, Web pages, images, and text clips. One of my tabs is labeled *Code Clips*. Here I have clips of programming scripts that I use in my software writing that are used frequently but are too long and complex to memorize (See figure 2.4).

If I am writing code that will access information from an online database to be placed in a Web page, I pop out the Code Clips drawer, click on the word **Access**, and it automatically pastes the programming script that will open a database directly into my program I am writing. There is also a link that runs a dictionary program on my computer. If I need to look up a word, I copy it into the clipboard, then pull out a drawer, double click on MacDICT, and definitions automatically pop up from a half-dozen dictionaries.

There is a similar program that I use on Windows computers called Phrase Express from **Bartels Media** (<http://www.phraseexpress.com>). This is a system tray application that when clicked, slides out a panel with links to text clips and software launches. Being digital means bringing your information and your tools together so that they are readily available to you as you work the information.

Investigative Strategies—Finding Witnesses

Global information is **connected** today in a way that it has never been in the past. Most of the billions of online documents available over the Internet are connected to other documents, which are connected to others, forming a global Web of information—an information universe. Finding information within this universe that helps you solve your problem is a challenge, but it involves a process of investigation more than mere technical practices. True Internet researchers are detectives, investigating a digital universe for answers and solutions. Like the criminal detective, they search for clues, find and organize evidence, and make a case.

When detectives investigate a crime, they are just as interested in witnesses as they are in physical evidence. This is why it is important that you not overlook the people on the Internet who might help in providing valuable information. We typically think of Web pages when we go to the Net for the answer to a question, but often people can provide much more valuable information. The parents of your students can be a good first place to look for digital witnesses. They are certainly an underutilized resource because of busy schedules. However, one of the most important benefits of wiring our schools is the conduit that it has formed between the classroom and the home. A parent whose profession, hobby, or travel experience might enhance a new unit is suddenly reachable through e-mail, instant messaging, or even Web-based teleconferencing.

Get to know who your students' parents are. "It takes a village ...", but we have to invite that village in. Use figure 2.5 as a model for a form for collecting information on potential Internet guest speakers during next year's open house or on an ongoing basis. It is also available as an editable file on this book's Web site (<http://landmark-project.com/redefining_literacy>).

Johnston Jones Middle School
Volunteer Form

Parent Name: _____   Student Name: _____

Parent Phone Number: _____
Parent E-mail Address: _____
IM Network and Screen Name: _____

Please check any topics on which you might be prepared to contribute.

| Sept | Ecosystems | ❏ | Feb | Landforms | ❏ |
| Nov | Energy | ❏ | Apr | Weather & Climate | ❏ |

I can interact with class by:		I can provide:	
Visiting the class	❏	Personal information	❏
Speaker phone	❏	Photos	❏
E-mail	❏	Computers/Slideshow	❏
Chat	❏	Video	❏
Video conference	❏	Access to other experts	❏

_____
Signed

Figure 2.5: Volunteer Form

Another strategy for locating potential virtual speakers for your classroom is to find a Web site that includes the information that you are teaching, presented in a way that is similar to the way that you teach it. Then, rather than (or in addition to) having students use the site, invite the Web master or author of the site to contribute to your lesson in some more direct way through e-mail or instant messenger.

Mailing lists are another potent source for experts to be invited, digitally, into your classroom (See figure 2.6). As an example, let's assume that you are a health teacher, looking for ways to convey to your students the importance of healthful living habits. It might be beneficial to find an online community of experts on nutrition or exercise and then use them as a resource for your students. However, be open to the idea that experts do not always come with credentials. Sometimes, the best expertise comes from experience; in this case, maybe people who are suffering from their poor habits of the past.

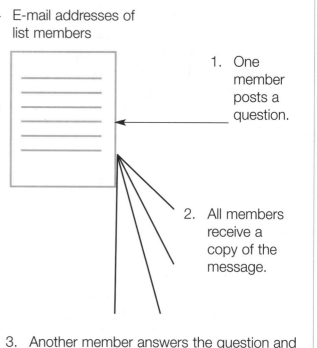

Through the Internet, people with similar interests and needs can create online communities where they can compare, share, inform, and develop ideas related to their mutual pursuits.

Technically, a mailing list is a list of e-mail addresses belonging to the members of the community. When one member sends a message to the list, copies of the message are automatically sent to all other members. When another member replies to the message, copies of the response are also sent out to all members.

The members of the list experience a group discussion through which problems are solved, questions are answered, and information is shared.

E-mail addresses of list members

1. One member posts a question.

2. All members receive a copy of the message.

3. Another member answers the question and all other members receive the answer.

Figure 2.6: Mailing Lists

One of the possible outcomes of poor health habits is heart disease. It is possible that there might be a mailing list that is devoted to support among people with heart disease, where they can share their experiences, problems, solutions, latest research, and other information that is mutually beneficial to the group. Might these people have something to share with your students? How might we locate such a group?

There are thousands of mailing lists on the Internet covering just about any topic that you could imagine, and probably some that you could not imagine. There are also a number of tools that can help you find mailing lists that discuss the topic you are looking for. We might try a tool called *Catalist* first. Catalist is like other search engines except that it searches for mailing lists instead of Web pages. It specifically searches for mailing lists that use the *Listserv* mailing list management software, a product of L-Soft, which also owns Catalist. It is important to note that Listserv is a highly sophisticated product that requires a fairly high degree of technical expertise to install and maintain. This is important because only organizations that can afford this level of expertise typically use Listserv (corporations, universities, hospitals, established non-profits, and so on), implying that these might be more serious mailing lists.

You visit **Catalist** (<http://www.lsoft.com/lists/list_q.html>) and enter the key term *heart disease* into the search box. After a moment one mailing list appears, entitled Congenital Heart Disease. If you are unsure about the definition of *congenital*, you quickly access an online dictionary from your personal digital information library and look it up, discovering that it means "existing at or dating from birth". You decide that this list is not related to your search for problems resulting from bad health practices.

Our problem is that the hits, or resulting list of finds, are too narrow. We need to broaden our scope to include more possible online communities to choose from. So we simplify our search term. Rather than entering *heart disease*, we shorten it to just *heart*.

This time we get 35 hits on a wider range of topics, some of which have nothing to do with health. But, from the descriptions that we receive, we learn that a number of the mailing lists are related to heart diseases and those who suffer from them. We select one of these lists, click the title, and learn some basic information including number of members of this list, how to reach the list archive, and instructions for joining the list. By clicking the Web **Archive Interface** link, we get a search tool that enables us to browse through messages that have already been posted by the members week by week, or enter a search term to access all messages that include that word or phrase. Entering the word *diet* returns hundreds of messages, each a possible source of information for your students.

To join the list, you are provided with an e-mail address and a join command. You simply address an e-mail message to the address provided, and paste the command (usually *subscribe [list name]*) into the body of the message. After sending the message, you receive a reply from the mailing list computer either welcoming you to the list or giving further instructions for confirming your registration.

In most cases, you would go ahead and join the list and start receiving copies of all of the messages posted by its members. However, the issues here are somewhat sensitive and personal, so it would be wise to seek permission from the owner of the list first. The owner's e-mail address is also provided. Here is how such a message might be written:

```
Dear List Owner,
I am a sixth-grade health teacher in North Carolina.
Part of my curriculum is to convey to my students
the importance of a healthy diet and exercise. I
would like to join your [list name] mailing list for
a three-week period and monitor the discussions for
tips, advice, and other information that may be
especially convincing to my students.

    Further, with your permission, I would like to
post up to three questions to the list seeking out
advice from heart patients that may effectively
```

```
impress on my sixth-grade students how critical it
is to take care of their health.
    I look forward to your reply.
Regards,
Janice Sneedley
Health Teacher, Johnston Middle School
Johnston, NC
<http://www.csd.k12.nc.us/sneedley6>
jsneedley@csd.k12.nc.us
```

Notice that this message is short, to the point, and describes clearly why I want to join the list and what I intend to do. Here are some other Web-based tools that you can use to locate mailing lists on the Internet based on topics that you are teaching or supporting.

Title	Location
Tile.Net	<http://www.tile.net/>
Publicly Accessible Mailing Lists	<http://paml.alastra.com/>
W3C Mailing-List Search Service	<http://www.w3.org/Search/Mail/Public/>
Mailing Lists archived by Ask ERIC	<http://www.askeric.org/Virtual/Listserv_/Archives/>
Yahoo!Groups	<http://www.yahoogroups.com/>

Figure 2.7: Other Mailing Lists

Investigative Strategies — Finding Evidence

If I were to continue our field trip through the evolving world of networked information, the next major achievement would be the **Search Engine**. This powerful and immensely valuable tool enables us to search for information through enormous online collections, sifting through billions of Web documents for specific words and phrases. With this seemingly magical tool at our disposal, it is important to understand exactly what is happening when we use a search engine to seek Web pages on a given topic.

First of all, search engines do not search the Internet, at least in the way that you might suspect. When searching a book for the answer to your question, you rarely scan the entire book. You scan the table of contents and index for references to the problem. Search engines also search indexes to find references to Web pages. These indexes can be huge, holding references to billions of Web pages, as is the case with **Google** (<http://www.google.com>). The indexes of other search engines can be small. Yahoo's directory index represents only a tiny fraction of what Google has. However, this does not mean that Google is better than Yahoo. It means that different search engines enable us to solve different kinds of problems. Sometimes it is more suitable to deal with 200 hits than with 400,000 hits.

Search Engine	A search engine scans an index for Web pages that include the words or phrases described in the search phrase.
Web Directory	A Web directory arranges Web pages from its index into a cascading series of menus, starting with general subjects, linking down to highly specialized subtopics.
Index Size	Indicates the amount of the Internet that is represented by the index, which is reflected by the number of hits you get. Large index search engines are not necessarily better than small index search engines.
Relevancy Ranking	This is how the search engine arranges the hits, identifying those Web pages that are probably most relevant to the problem you are trying to solve. There are a variety of ways to do this including: number of occurrences of the keyword, where the keyword occurs in the Web page, whether the keyword is in the page title, other Web pages that link to the considered page.
Freshness	How quickly the search engine is able to find and include new Web pages. This will indicate how current the hits will be.
Boolean	A language for posting questions to a search engine. Involves connectors and punctuation to describe relationships between words in the search phrase.

Figure 2.8: Search Engine Vocabulary

It is also helpful to understand that most search engines create their own indexes. If we had to rely on people to add all of the Web pages to a search engine's index, we would be woefully behind in representing the content of the Internet in our Web searches. These enormous indexes are grown and maintained by semi-intelligent software agents. Before your imagination takes over, let me explain that these agents, often called spiders, are merely small pieces of software that are programmed to wander through the WWW, following Web links in much the same way that you browse through links as you surf the Net. These spider programs record the links that they encounter and when they find a hyperlink that has not been recorded, they follow it to its target page. The spider then checks the page to see if it is already known by the search engine. If not, the spider sends all of the pertinent information about the page back to the search engine, where it is added to the index.

This is an important concept to understand because it explains why, when you use a search engine, you often receive a large number of hits that seem to be completely unrelated to your topic. Search engines are wonderfully powerful tools, but they cannot think. They search for strings of characters, not meaning. They do the best that they can to put the most relevant pages at the top of your list of hits, but they do not truly understand what you want.

Examining the sites, comparing the meaning of information, and making judgments and decisions on which information is valuable and which is not is still the job of people. It is a skill that we learn by doing and sharing with others. Net research is something that

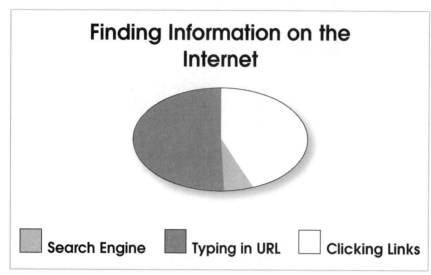

Finding Information on the Internet

■ Search Engine   ■ Typing in URL   □ Clicking Links

Figure 2.9: How People Find Information

educators should be doing every day, continually building knowledge and teaching resources in a personal digital information library, and sharing with appropriate colleagues what has been found.

The truth is that search engines are surprisingly under-utilized tools. According to Danny Sullivan of Search Engine Watch, only 7 to 8% of Web destinations are reached using a search engine (See figure 2.9). By comparison, 52% are reached by entering the URL, and 41% by clicking links (<http://www.searchenginewatch.com/sereport/02/02-nav.html>). This indicates that there is a great deal of valuable information that is not being used because people do not understand or use search engines. Much more information about these tools and their use can be found at two rich Web sites: **Search Engine Watch** (<http://www.searchenginewatch.com>) and **Search Engine Showdown** (<http://www.searchengineshowdown.com>).

Most of the readers of this book have used search engines to find information on the Internet. You have typed keywords into your favorite search engine and then scanned through the first 20 or 30 Web pages out of the tens or hundreds of thousands of hits, or you may simply settle for one of the first five or six pages that appear in the list. Some of you may have even be improving your results by using Boolean or search math to refine your search phrases. Search strategy, however, is far deeper than knowing when to use AND, OR, and NOT.

I am going to describe this strategy, but first we will walk through the scenario of a middle-school student conducting Internet research in order to complete an assignment. Her name is Suzette, and her teacher has given her class the following assignment.

> It is 2050, and we are terraforming the planet Mars. Scientists are identifying animals from our planet to migrate to Mars and are especially interested in grazing animals. Your assignment is to select a grazing animal and submit a report that describes the animal and how it interacts with other organisms in its ecosystem.

Suzette has two problems:

1. Select a grazing animal for her report.
2. Collect information about the animal and how it interacts with other organisms.

She starts, as most of us do, with a large index search engine such as Google, entering *grazing animals* as her search term. Suzette receives 280,000 hits. She scans the first page or two of hits discovering Web sites on grazing terminology, official documents from the U.S. Environmental Protection Agency, and books on the management of domestic farm animals in the Netherlands. Although some of these pages might be helpful later, they do not help Suzette with her first problem: selecting a grazing animal.

Our student researcher then decides that she needs Web pages that have more general information on grazing animals, so she decides to use Yahoo. Although this search tool contains a powerful search engine, Suzette decides to use its Web directory to find more general information by category. The difference between a Web directory and search engine is that the directory stores what it knows about the Internet by subject, topic, and subtopic. You start with a page of general subjects (Business, Computers, News, Arts, Reference, and so on) and select the subject that comes closest to solving your problem. This produces a list of topics that belong to your selected subject. Clicking the appropriate topic usually produces a list of subtopics. The benefits are that the final list of Web sites is short and the sites are typically of a more general nature.

Suzette selects **Science** as the initial subject and then **Animals, Insects, & Pets** from the following list of topics. Among the subtopics that appear, Suzette selects **Mammals** since most of the grazing animals she knows of have hair and bear their young alive. However, the following list of subtopics does not include grazing mammals, nor does it include links that might help identify grazing animals. Our student researcher rethinks again, deciding that she needs to go even more general, seeking a site that includes all animals. Such a site might have information to help her select only grazing animals.

Suzette backs out from the **Mammals** page to **Animals, Insects, & Pets**. She scrolls down to the listing of Web sites on the page (Yahoo directory pages list subtopics of the current topic and then links to Web sites that are appropriate) and selects Animal Diversity Web because it probably has information about the animals that will help her solve her first problem.

From this Web site, she can select animals by class (mammals, birds, amphibians, and so on) and subclass (prototheria, metatheria, eutheria, and so on). Again, not very helpful, but this detail of information indicates a fairly rich Web site, so she switches strategy, again returning to Google. Here she enters *grazing* into the search box followed by *site:animaldiversity.ummz.umich.edu*, the URL of the Animal Diversity site. By adding the word *site* followed by a colon and the Web address, Google will search for pages with grazing only within the Animal Diversity site. This was an especially good strategy because not only did Google report pages on grazing animals but also pages on animals that are affected by grazing animals. This will be helpful in solving her second problem as well.

As Suzette reviews a number of the grazing animals, she discovers that certain birds, fish, and mollusks are also considered grazers. This idea challenges her previous perception of grazing animals, enriching the concept in her mind. This is a good and useful byproduct of searching the Internet. You nearly always learn something new.

Suzette selects the Saiga Antelope partly because it is so ugly it is cute, but mostly because it lives in an ecosystem that is in flux. Its habitat was closely regulated by the Soviet Union. However, after the nations of that former state separated, the smaller, less wealthy individual countries could not enforce regulations and the antelope came under attack by poachers, was affected by the decline of predators, and came into more frequent contact with domestic grazing animals, causing the spread of disease.

Suzette continues her research by entering *saiga* and *antelope* into Google. She receives over a thousand hits and she realizes that these are pages that have *saiga* somewhere and *antelope* somewhere, not necessarily together. She adjusts her search to *"saiga antelope"*. The quotation marks force Google to find only pages that include the phrase *saiga antelope*—the two words together. This decreases the number of hits to only 882.

Our student researcher begins scanning the pages, finding a great deal of information about the saiga, and also a couple of sites about the animal's environment, each of which includes the word *ecosystem*. There are other pages mixed in, especially advertisements for books about animals. She feels that what she needs is among the 882 Web pages, but rather than waste time continuing to scan this many pages, she decides to refine her search one more time: *"saiga antelope" ecosystem -book*.

This final search phrase asks for pages that have the term or phrase *saiga antelope* and also the word *ecosystem* somewhere on the page. It will, however, omit any pages that have the word *book*. The book omission is signaled by the minus sign in front of the word *book*. The result is 102 hits with just the information she seeks.

Searching the Internet is a process. It is an investigation, an act of finding clues and evidence and refining your strategy based on those clues. I hope that the scenario above has helped you to understand this process and to understand how this process can be instructional on its own. Because we are using information to navigate the Internet, each adaptation of our search strategy leads to a new understanding of the topic and the knowledge that surrounds it.

Another way to teach the search process is to use a model called S.E.A.R.C.H. This is an acronym that represents the steps of using a process approach to searching the Net (See figure 2.10).

Start	Small and Simple. It may not be helpful to start with Google, which could deliver millions of hits on the first search. Start with a small index search engine such as Yahoo. Examine a sampling of hits identifying words common in the relevant resources and words common in the less than relevant Web pages.
Edit	Use the words identified in the previous step to edit your search phrase. Use Boolean or *Search Math* as the grammar of your search phrase.
Advance	Advance to a large database search engine, such as Google. Enter the *edited* search phrase and examine a sampling of hits, identifying more words that are common in pages that help you solve your problem and pages that are not relevant.
Refine	Refine your search phrase using the words identified in your *advance* search.
Cycle	Cycle back and advance again.
Harvest	Harvest the resources that were identified during your searches. This is an ongoing process.

Figure 2.10: The SEARCH Process

At the heart of the process is the continuing cycle of searching, examining the information (clues and evidence), refining the search strategy, and searching again. With each pass, you learn more about the topic. You also become exposed to different types of information.

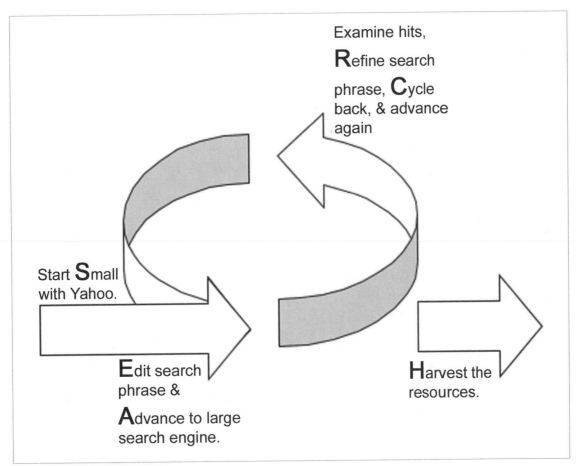

Figure 2.11: The SEARCH Cycle

You may have expected general Web pages but encountered tabular data describing the topic, or images. You may even find video and sound files or even virtual reality files. Each of these unexpected types of information will enrich your knowledge about the topic at hand.

Investigative Strategies — Search Logs

As students are conducting their research, it is important that they think about what they are searching for, what they are finding, and how they are adjusting their search strategies. One way of assuring that they think about their search is to ask them to keep a search log. Maintaining a search log will make the search process more tedious, but having students write down their evolving strategies will help them to see it as exactly that, an evolving and growing strategy. A search log should ask students to identify the goal of their research and the initial search term or phrase. Then, with each search, they should record the words that they find to be common in useful Web pages that appear (attractors) and words that are common in pages that are not useful (rejectors). Then the student researchers should record the refinements that they make to their search phrase. In addition to causing students to think more about their search strategies, keeping a search log also enables them to look back at their developing strategies and retry alternative phrases. See figure 2.12 for the log that Suzette kept as she conducted her research on grazing animals. A blank version of this log form is available on the book's Web site (<http://landmark-project.com/redefining_literacy>).

Search Tool	Search Phrase
☐ Yahoo ☐ Alta Vista ☒ Google ☐ Yahooligans ☐ Lycos Other:	grazing animals
Comments: Received more than 280,000 hits, and most of the first ones were too specific. Will try for a more general search using Yahoo.	
☒ Yahoo ☐ Alta Vista ☐ Google ☐ Yahooligans ☐ Lycos Other:	Science/Animals, Insects, & Pets/Mammals
Comments: No subtopics for grazing animals. Must broaden search by dropping back out to all animals.	
☒ Yahoo ☐ Alta Vista ☐ Google ☐ Yahooligans ☐ Lycos Other:	Science/Animals, Insects, & Pets
Comments: Found page with information about animals and how they are different. Should have information about grazing animals. Animal Diversity Web.	
☐ Yahoo ☐ Alta Vista ☒ Google ☐ Yahooligans ☐ Lycos Other:	grazing site:animaldiversity.ummz.umich.edu
Comments: Received 117 pages in Animal Diversity with the word "grazing." Very good information. Selecting Saiga Antelope.	
☐ Yahoo ☐ Alta Vista ☒ Google ☐ Yahooligans ☐ Lycos Other:	saiga antelope
Comments: 1,360 hits. Not many useful in first few pages. New strategy.	
☐ Yahoo ☒ Alta Vista ☐ Google ☐ Yahooligans ☐ Lycos Other:	"saiga antelope"
Comments: Down to 882 hits. Many pages about saiga. Also many pages about book about saiga. Found one page with information about ecosystem. New strategy.	
☐ Yahoo ☒ Alta Vista ☐ Google ☐ Yahooligans ☐ Lycos Other:	"saiga antelope" ecosystem —book
Comments: Down to 102 hits. Pages about saiga environment and ecosystem. Bingo!	

Figure 2.12: Internet Search Evaluation Tool

Finally, search logs can easily be kept on paper. However, it makes much more sense if students can complete them digitally, as a word processing file. It saves time, in that students are able to copy and paste words and terms, rather than writing them on paper. In addition, they can edit their evolving search phrases more easily with the word processor and can then copy and paste the text directly into the search engine. Anything that can be done to ease the labor of conducing research will improve the success of the task.

Investigative Strategies — Search Language

Some readers may have been involved in computers and education long enough to remember *Dialog*. This was one of the earliest online information services and was used a great deal by schools. The problem with Dialog was that it charged by the minute, and the fees were not insignificant. As a result, the process for searching its database involved spending time composing, editing, and refining your search phrase before even touching the computer.

After assuring that your search phrase was complete, you dialed up, logged in, typed in your search phrase, received the list of hits, printed them out, and logged off as quickly as you could. This provided schools with access to information that was not available otherwise, but it was not a good model for the kind of research we conduct today. With the Internet, research is a more interactive process, where you begin with a simple strategy and increasingly refine your search phrase based on what you find and learn.

This interaction requires that we communicate with the search tool in order to define what we are looking for. It requires a language. With Dialog (and some search engines today) the language for posing our search questions is called Boolean. This powerful set of rules and syntax enables you to describe the information you want and how it relates to other information. For instance, you are looking for information about Native Americans in the state of Ohio. You decide what words will probably appear in the Web pages that hold your information and enter those words. As an example, you might enter the following search phrase: *native americans indians ohio*.

The results are Web pages about native everything, American patriotism, all things Indian, everything you could imagine about the state of Ohio, and a slew of Web pages about the Cleveland Indians baseball team—about five million hits on Google. You clearly need to refine your search phrase (strategy), and you do this by describing the relation between these bits of information.

For instance, *native* and *americans* must be together as a phrase in order to have the meaning we are looking for. So we put quotation marks around this phrase: *"native americans" indians ohio*.

We know that sometimes the reference will be to *native americans* and sometimes it will be *indians*. So we insert a connector between the two words, *OR* (all caps): *"native americans" OR indians ohio*.

Searching for Native Americans or Indians is a separate issue from the state, so that sub-phrase is placed in parentheses and *ohio* is connected with an *AND*, indicating that it must be a part of the pages that are reported: *("native americans" OR indians) AND ohio*.

Finally, to remove references to the baseball team, we add a *NOT* connector and the phrase *Cleveland Indians* in quotation marks: *("native americans" OR indians) AND ohio NOT "cleveland indians"*.

The results are Web pages that mention *Native Americans* or *Indians* along with *Ohio*, but do not mention the *Cleveland Indians* ball team—about 13,000 hits.

In review, Boolean uses the following conventions:

- Quotation marks around phrases that have unique meaning,
- AND separating terms that must both appear in the returned Web pages,
- OR separating terms that either of which must appear in the returned pages,
- NOT preceding words or terms that must not appear in the returned pages.

Although this might seem complicated, it is not. Boolean is, however, difficult to explain, and for this reason, most Internet search engines have switched to a language that I call *Search Math*. It is not quite as powerful as Boolean, but Search Math is much easier to explain. In Search Math,

- all connectors are assumed to be AND.
- phrases are created with quotation marks, in the same way as Boolean.
- some of the search engines will accept OR as a connector.
- if there is a word or phrase that should not appear in the search, then it is preceded by a minus symbol (-) with no space between the word and symbol.

The Boolean phrase that we constructed above would be entered in search math as: *"native americans"* OR *indians* +*ohio* -*"cleveland indians"*.

Each search engine has its own set of conventions for composing your search phrase, and they change frequently. For this reason, I will not report them here. However, Greg Notess keeps an up-to-date chart listing the features of individual search engines on his Web site, Search Engine Showdown. His feature chart is at <http://www.searchengineshowdown.com/features>.

Thus far, we have only sought out Web pages with most any type of information. There are many search tools and many of them search for specific types of information. See figure 2.13 for a list of various search tools arranged by their specialty.

Investigative Strategy — Evaluating the Information

One of the most important shifts that has taken place in our society, and one that has gone by almost unnoticed, is a move from a broadcast model of content delivery to a multicast model. During most of the twentieth century media was generated and published by a few powerful entities: publishers, radio and TV broadcasters, and the movie and music industries. We, the consumers, purchased our news, entertainment, and knowledge from this monarchy of providers because it was impractical to produce our own media.

It is important to note that in the span of human history, this feudal approach to information sharing was fairly recent. Throughout most of human history, information was shared around the campfire, in the marketplace, or the town square. Gutenberg's printing press changed things with the production of relatively cheap books, causing an enormous increase in the sharing of knowledge and stories and a globalization of ideas. It also created a unique relationship between media producers and media consumers.

General Search Engines

Google	<http://www.google.com/>
Alta Vista	<http://www.altavista.com/>
All The Web (FAST)	<http://www.alltheweb.com/>
Yahoo	<http://www.yahoo.com/>
Lycos	<http://www.lycos.com/>
Ask Jeeves	<http://www.askjeeves.com/>

News Search Engines

Alta Vista News	<http://news.altavista.com/>
Daypop	<http://www.daypop.com/>
Moreover	<http://www.moreover.com/news/>
Net2one	<http://www.net20ne.com/>

Multimedia Search Engines

Lycos Pictures & Sound	<http://multimedia.lycos.com/>
FAST	<http://multimedia.alltheweb.com/>
Ditto	<http://www.ditto.com/>
Streamsearch	<http://www.streamsearch.com/>
Speechbot	<http://speechbot.research.compaq.com/>

Kid-Friendly Search Tools

Ask Jeeves for Kids	<http://www.ajkids.com/>
Yahooligans	<http://www.yahooligans.com/>
KidsClick!	<http://sunsite.berkeley.edu/KidsClick!/>
CyberSleuth Kids	<http://cybersleuth-kids.com/>

Figure 2.13: Search Engines

One of the qualities of this relationship was the fact that our information was highly filtered, protecting us from extreme or fringe ideas. With notable exceptions, media was aimed at a common denominator of reader in order to garner the most consumers and income. This trend increased as reading literacy increased — the literati of the 19th century becoming, in itself, a fringe group.

Because of this layer of filtering provided by producers of textbooks and other educational materials, teachers have been cushioned from inappropriate and harmful information, and it relieved us from the responsibilities of evaluating and selecting content for instruction. The information was packaged for us. All we had to do was deliver it.

Today, the relationship between information producer and consumer is changing. We are all becoming information producers and distributors, and through our bookmarks and online bookmark services, we are all becoming librarians. At the same time that this is providing unprecedented freedom of expression and a wealth of content, it is also threatening the comfort of having appropriate information selected for us. One example of how people are beginning to express their ideas in mass is a growing phenomena called *Blogging*. Anyone with access to the Web can create a blog, short for Web Log, and as a result can establish a Web presence where he or she can add and edit content. A blog is more like a diary or journal than anything else. You add text and sometimes images on a regular basis, and the entire content is stored as part of the page. CNN Headline News reported that there were somewhere between 200,000 and 500,000 blog sites in September 2002 (Boese <http://www.cnn.com/2002/SHOWBIZ/09/20/hln.hot.buzz.blog>). To create your own blog site:

1. Go to one of the free blogging services:
   - <http://www.blog-city.com>
   - <http://www.blogger.com>
2. Click on a sign-up link to create a free account
3. Fill in the Web form and agree to conditions
4. Start publishing

Once you have your blog, you can publish to your heart's content and have your ideas, beliefs, and passions available to a global audience.

What threatens our comfort as educators is the fact that if publishing is free or nearly free, then the filtering layer disappears. People publish not merely for profit, but because they want to share their own ideas and for their own reasons. Determining the validity of the information now rests exclusively on the consumer, and in a time when information drives nearly all aspects of our societies, the skills required to evaluate information—to expose the information—are absolutely critical to success today and in the future.

Large Idea!

...the skills required to evaluate information—to expose the truth—are absoultely critical to success today and in the future.

The government response to this challenge has been to require schools to install technology-based systems to filter out information that is in any way objectionable or dangerous to students. Although this solution makes a great deal of sense on the surface, filtering software does not solve the problem and even exacerbates the situation in important ways.

First of all, filters are not 100% successful. The Henry J. Kaiser Family Foundation recently conducted and published a study called "See No Evil: How Internet Filters Affect the Search for Online Health Information" (Rideout <http://www.kff.org/content/2002/3294/Internet_Filtering_exec_summ.pdf>), in which it analyzed the success of six filtering products that are used widely by schools and libraries. Using three standard settings for filtering (least restrictive, intermediate, and most restrictive), the study found that only 1.4% of all sites associated with health issues were blocked under the least restrictive setting. However, at the most restrictive setting, 24% of the health sites were blocked. When looking at sites on controversial issues related to health, such as "safe sex," the study found that a full 9% of the sites were blocked at the least restrictive setting, and 50% blocked at the most restrictive setting.

To further confuse the issues, when testing how well the filtering products block pornographic sites, only about 90% of the sites were blocked, regardless of the setting (87% at least restrictive, 90% at intermediate settings, and 91% at most restrictive). It is clear that filtering software alone does not solve the problem, but our response has been to settle back into our assumptions of safety, as we struggle to prepare our students for their reading and math tests. We think that the problem has been solved because we think that it is an infrastructure problem. Addressing inappropriate information on the Internet is not a technology issue, it is a literacy issue.

One of my favorite scenarios finds a middle-school child researching the Civil Rights movement, specifically Martin Luther King. Conducting his research at home, and away from the protection of the school's filtering software, he finds the Web site **Martin Luther King, Jr.: A True Historical Examination** (<http://www.martinlutherking.org>). He sees and begins to read what is a polished, well organized, and professional looking Web document. However, if this student has been taught to evaluate information, which means being willing to ask questions about the answers he finds, then he becomes immediately suspicious of this document. The clue is the fact that there is no reference on the page to the author of this document or the publishing organization. This is not a condition that should automatically disqualify the document from use, but it is a reason to become suspicious and investigate further. Again, using information in the digital world requires us to be detectives—and it can be fun.

Our student, understanding something about how the Web works, does find the text *Contact the Web Master: Click Here*. The *Click Here* is hyperlinked to the author's e-mail address. Our researcher knows that if he clicks the link, his e-mail program will start, addressing a new message to the Web master of the page. If he clicks the link with his right mouse button instead, and selects from the pop-up menu, *Copy Link Location*, the author's e-mail address is copied into the computer's clipboard. He pastes the address into a blank text document (SimpleText, NotePad, or TextEdit) and discovers an e-mail URL: mailto:vincent.breeding@stormfront.org.

This is an e-mail URL because the prefix is *mailto:*, rather than the Web URL prefix of *http://*. We discover that the owner of the address is Vincent Breeding, and the domain of the organization that is providing him with e-mail access is *stormfront.org*.

We now have some clues about the origins of this Web page. For instance, we can enter the owner's name into a search engine and learn more about what he has written and what other people have written about him. A search in Google (<http://www.google.com>) reveals more than 800 hits. Also, using a text processor, our student can remove the *mailto:* prefix from the e-mail URL and replace it with the Web prefix, *http://*. Then he replaces the user's e-mail name and the *at* (@) symbol with *www(dot)*. The result is a Web URL, <http://www.stormfront.org>, for the organization providing the author with e-mail.

Our digital investigator then copies the Web URL into his computer's clipboard and pastes it into the address bar of his browser. The page that loads tells all. It is a white supremacist organization.

Students are literate in the traditional sense, and in the sense on which students are being tested today, if they can read and understand the text in front of them. Can we call them literate in a twenty-first century sense if all they can do is read the Web page in front of them?

Large Idea!

Addressing inappropriate information on the Internet is not a technology issue, it is a literacy issue.

Literacy must be redefined and expanded to address a new information world that is larger in scope and yet smaller in access. We would be better off not teaching children to read if we are not helping them to critically evaluate what they are reading. Students must learn to be suspicious of information, to ask questions, and to be ready to defend the information that they use and build with.

Investigative Strategy — Asking Questions

Selecting information from the global Internet requires the investigative technique of a newspaper reporter as much as a detective. As mentioned earlier, literacy in the twenty-first century includes a willingness to ask questions about the answers you find. In writing a news article reporters try to answer five questions, or the five Ws: **Who**, **What**, **When**, **Where**, and **Why**. These Ws make a very effective basis for evaluating information available to us on the Internet for the same reasons that they have served reporters. They tend to tell the whole story.

Before we discuss these five questions, it is important to create a context for these questions that is useful to student learning. It relates to the nature of the assignments we give our students. If the assignment is to write a report about South Africa, then almost anything goes. There is no compelling reason for the student to seriously evaluate the information he or she finds beyond determining that it is **about South Africa**. A newspaper editor would not ask a reporter to write a piece about South Africa unless there was a *story* in it, unless it impacted on people in some way. Teachers might think of themselves as the editors-in-chief of their classrooms, asking students to produce pieces that result in a *story* that will impact people in some way. If the student is asked to write a report that supports the continued financial support for that nation or discontinuance of funding, then that assignment has a goal. Not only is this a more authentic assignment, but it also gives the student an excellent basis for evaluating the information that he or she finds that supports the report. Students ask the question, "How does this information help me accomplish my goal?"

When addressing the **who** part of our evaluation of an information source, we are seeking information about the author within the context of our goal. "What is it about the author or the publishing organization that helps me support continued financial aid, or discontinuing assistance?" Deep within this question is an implied question, "Is this information the truth?" We will discuss truth later, but for now, is it evident (is there evidence) that the author or publishing organization has expertise or experience in the subject being considered?

If you have the name, or even the e-mail address of the author, there is much you can do to investigate the source of your information. Use the same Internet search engine that connected you with the information in order to investigate the author. When you enter the author's name (inside quotes) or even the e-mail address into a large search engine, you will learn more about the author, access other documents he or she has published, and learn what other people have to say about the person — each adding to your body of evidence.

Another question to ask is, "**What**?" What is the content you have found? What does it mean? How does it agree or disagree with other sources of information on the same topic? Some sub-questions to ask are:

- Does the information affect you on an emotional level?
- Does the information promote anger or ill will toward other people or their ideas?

- Does the information make significant use of multimedia in communicating an idea?
- Does the information in any way threaten you or make you feel ill at ease?

An affirmative to any of these sub-questions should raise a flag of suspicion. It does not mean that the information should be discarded, but it does indicate that someone is trying to convince you of an idea that may be difficult to sell without a clear and logical consideration of facts. Continue to investigate.

In terms of the assignment, does the nature of the information help you accomplish your goal? How does the information look? Does its format (prose, data, image, animation, video) help you accomplish your goal?

"**When**" is a tricky question. It is a critical question, but we should not automatically assume that the more recent document is necessarily the better one. It depends on the goal. If the student is investigating America's move toward war in 1941, documents dated at that time may be the most valuable and critical to the assignment, under most circumstances. The evidence the student seeks is, "How does the publishing or revision date of the document help accomplish the goal of the assignment?" "In what way does it contribute to the story or the position?"

It can be difficult to determine the date of an online document if the author has not posted it as part of the page. However, one way to determine date is to use **The Way Back Machine** (<http://www.archive.org>). This Web service is dedicated to archiving the World Wide Web. It periodically takes photographs, so to speak, of Web pages and archives those pages in its library in a way that allows us to see what those pages looked like and what they said over the months and years. For instance, I am considering Web pages about the nation of Syria and have found a site called SyriaGate. The page does not post any dates for its initial publishing or subsequent revisions. So I go to **The Way Back Machine** and enter the travel site's URL: <http://www.syriagate.com>.

Upon clicking the submit button, I receive a list of dates on which that particular page was archived. The most recent, as of the writing of this book, was on June 5, 2002—just more than a year ago. I can click that date to see what the page said then and compare with the content one year later. There are 36 other dates going back to November 28, 1999, so even when I cannot establish the current date of a document, I can find reference points. If you are using Netscape Navigator as your browser, you can select Page Info from the View menu and learn more about the page, often including the date that the file was created and last modified.

When writing a newspaper article, the reporter considers geography when answering the "**Where**" question. Even though geography may be a factor critical to the goal of the assignment, the student should also consider where the author or publishing organization sits within a political or ideological spectrum. Is there anything about the author that would lead you to believe that his or her information is less than true, in terms of accomplishing your goals, or is the author attempting to manipulate the truth in some way to accomplish an agenda? Related to "**where**" is "**why**." What does the author have to gain by publishing this information? Is there any evidence that the author would gain from reporting something less than the truth?

In the scenario with the Martin Luther King site, we learned by investigating the organization that provided the author with an e-mail address that chances were high that the author was influenced by ideologies that were dramatically to the right on the political spectrum.

The form in figure 2.14 might be helpful in giving students a structure for asking these questions. This form can also be downloaded from the "Learning & Literacy" Web site (<http://landmark-project.com/redefining_literacy>). In addition, there is a Web version of this form at <http://landmark-project.com/evaluation/evalform_1.php3>.

Investigative Strategy — Defend Your Information

I want to carry our detective metaphor a little bit further. Our students have sought their information, acting like detectives, searching for clues and evidence about the topic they are researching, refining their search strategies, and uncovering information sources for their project. They have investigated their findings, looking for the truth, bias, and validity. They must next defend their information. In the Information Age, information has value, but that value must be defended. Students, and the rest of us, should be able to provide evidence that information is true, without truth-altering bias, and appropriate to the task at hand.

Ask students to defend their information. In fact, hold a jury trial for student information. Ask them, as an assignment, to answer a question by researching the Internet. The more controversial the issue is, the better the assignment, though you must be careful about the degree of controversy you want to introduce to your class. One example might be, "Should the United States continue its manned space exploration programs?" Inform the students that they will not be graded on their answers, but on how well they can defend the information they use to support their answers. Part of the assignment is to be able to provide evidence that the information they found is:

Large Idea!

In the Information Age, information has value, but that value must be defended.

■ True
  • Does it agree with other sources?
  • Is the author or publishing organization an authority?
  • Is the information's truth constant and dependable?
■ Without truth-altering bias
  • What might the author or publishing organization have to gain by reporting the information?
  • Is it in their interest to alter the truth in any way that would impact on the question?
■ Applicable to the question being addressed
  • In what way(s) does the information apply to the question?
  • In what way(s) does the question influence the truth of the information?

You can carry this activity all the way to a mock courtroom with a judge, jury, prosecuting and defending attorneys, and courtroom reporters, or you can simply institute a practice of questioning sources in your classroom. Invite students to question the information they are being taught. Challenge them to defend or prosecute sources that are brought in, including textbooks. If the teacher is asked to back up the information he or she is sharing, then we are doing simply what we should be doing—teaching in the twenty-first century.

Project Title:	
Project Goal:	

Resource Name:	
Resource Location (URL):	
Author:	
Publishing Organization:	

What aspects of the author or publishing organization help you accomplish your goal?

When published or last revised?	

What aspects of the publishing date help you accomplish your goal?

What is the information?

What aspects of the information help you accomplish your goal?

Figure 2.14: Net Evaluation Form

Large Idea!

Conclusion

Exposing the Information is the longest and most involved section of this book. Although each of the twenty-first century literacies covered in this book equip us as lifelong learners, exposing the information is probably the most useful as a learning literacy. If you attend educational technology conferences, you hear a lot about online courses. Providing instruction over the networks solves many problems related to educating a nation and world. However, a majority of the distance learning that people will be engaged in will be of a more casual nature. It will simply mean using the network (electronic or otherwise) to learn what you need to know, in order to do what you need to do — right now!

Being literate in the twenty-first century means that we are beginning to think beyond the place we can see and the momentary time we experience. It means that we increasingly identify ourselves by what we know, and that what we know springs from a vast, dynamic, growing, global, increasingly accessible, and powerfully searchable world of information—and of people with whom we can share that information.

To take advantage of this digital realm, we must be plugged in, both literally and figuratively. We must have access to the devices through which digital information is provided, and the knowledge and skills to use those devices in order to interact with that world happily and productively.

Action Items

Directors of Technology

- Create a standard page with the district's banner that includes links to appropriate search tools and other Web-based information searching resources so that the page becomes, among other things, a doorway to the global Internet. This page can then be linked to by school, media center, and special project sites in the district.
- Establish policies regarding access to dangerous information that emphasize proactive guidance, appropriate instructional practices, and observation and evaluation of student use; and policies that address filtering and blocking technologies required by the government.
- Configure all systems so that each teacher (and student if possible) can establish personal information digital libraries that follow the person from station to station.
- Work with other curriculum leaders to integrate proper research and self-teaching into classroom activities that are consistent with twenty-first century technologies and culture.

Principals

- Integrate into your teacher evaluation system the expectation that teachers will integrate digital information materials into their lessons on a daily basis.

- To the greatest degree possible, expect students to turn in their assignments digitally — on disk or tape, or over the Internet. They should be producing digital products, not just paper.
- Arrange computer and Internet facilities in your school in a way that offers the most access to the most people possible, and in a way that affords flexibility in their use.
- Arrange supervised after-hours access to computers for students and families who do not have convenient access at home.

Media Specialists

- Collect and maintain a list of local residents with expertise who will make themselves available to classrooms for either face-to-face interaction with students or via Internet communication (e-mail, chat, message board, or video conference).
- Maintain a Web site that offers links to Internet resources related to topics being studied in your teachers' classrooms. Treat these pages as reserve lists.
- Establish and use a personal digital information library. If it is not useful, then reorganize it and try again. Help teachers in establishing their own personal digital information libraries.
- Create inviting and comfortable stations for students to conduct research — knowledge gardens.

School Tech Facilitators

- Map the school's curriculum in a way that you and the media specialist have access to what is currently being taught by each teacher.
- Facilitate an ongoing, but casual, professional development environment that encourages teachers to discuss, share, and ask about digital teaching (and learning) resources available on the Net and elsewhere.
- Attend all department or grade-level meetings and be ready to suggest strategies and resources that reflect a twenty-first century literacy.
- With each lesson that you teach, do a quick search of a news search tool to add something that is current.
- Establish a mailing list or group messaging system and announce new resources and research tools to the teachers and other instructional staff. As much as possible, be able to forward such messages to specific categories (Social Studies Teachers, for example) of educators.

Teachers

- Maintain a list of your students' parents with areas of expertise, hobbies, and travels. Make sure that you have e-mail addresses for these parents for convenient communication.
- Establish and use a personal digital information library. If it is not useful, then reorganize it and try again.
- Make the Internet a part of every assignment or lesson. Integrate digital information into everything that you do.

- With each lesson that you teach, do a quick search of a news search tool to add something that is current.

Students

- With each research assignment that you receive, do a significant amount of the research over the Internet. If your teacher will not accept Internet research, ask why, and wait for a good answer that relates to your future.
- Search not only for information in the form of text, but also images, animations, sound, and video.
- Turn in as many of your assignments as you can in digital format (disk, CD-ROM, over the Internet). If your teacher will not accept them, ask why and wait for a good answer that relates to your future.

Parents

- Make sure that each of your children has access to a computer connected to the Internet. This does not mean that each child should have his or her own computer, but that each child has access.
- When they are conducting research, sit and watch. If you have experience, help. Ask them to explain what they are finding and how it applies to what they are learning in class.
- If your children's teachers are not accepting assignments turned in digitally or limit the use of the Internet and other digital resources in their assignments, ask why and wait for a good answer.
- When teachers do engage in activities that make creative and exciting use of digital information, share it with other parents and community members. Send an e-mail to the teacher commending the teacher for his or her vision and copy it to the principal, media specialist, and school tech facilitator.

3 Employing the Information

The early part of my life was spent pretty squarely in the middle of the twentieth century. Upon leaving high school, a majority of the students I went to school with took employment in one of the 16 mills that defined my hometown or the factories in the larger towns and cities of the area. It had been that way for many decades, and any indications that things would change within our generation were far from our consideration. We, including myself, made yarn, thread, tires, oil filters, and chainsaws. The raw materials that we worked with were fibers, magnesium, steel, plastic, and tin. Our job was to fashion these raw materials into products that had value.

I worked for nearly a year in a factory machine shop. Because I had taken drafting when I was in high school and could read a blue print, I was quickly promoted to a supervisory position called "Setup Man." My section made the carburetors for chainsaws. When I received an order for a different carburetor to be installed in a different model of chainsaw, I found the blueprints in a file cabinet and used this guide and my tools to literally disassemble the manufacturing machines in my section and reassemble them so that they would drill the holes to the correct depths, set the screws, and mill and sand the surfaces to the described clearances. I then instructed the operators on how to run the newly rebuilt machines and supervised their work.

Today, the person with this responsibility may access part specifications from a network, rather than a file cabinet. He or she converts those specifications into a set of instructions or a program, using special software on a computer. Finally, these instructions are uploaded through a network to a control computer that repurposes a robot to make the new carburetor. There are no machine operators, and the person who programs the robot may not even work on the plant floor. They may not even be in the same state.

During most of the twenty-first century, manufacturing will be accomplished almost exclusively by machines. They are fast, tireless, cheap, and expendable. The information that drives these machines will be constructed, managed, and communicated by people. The chainsaw carburetors will probably continue to be made of steel, but in the Information Age, information is the raw material with which people will work. We must teach our children to build with information.

When I grew up, we had one television that the entire family shared, and it was able to tune into three networks and one independent station. We had a choice of four video media sources, and what we watched at a certain time was determined by their programming. If you wanted to watch a program, you had to be at your TV when the station or network aired that program.

Today, there are four televisions in my house, each connected to a cable service that provides access to hundreds of channels of video content

Large Idea!

... in the Information Age, information is the raw material with which people will work.

(and even more of audio content). Through that same cable line, I have access to the Internet with unimaginable access to text, audio, video, and animation that I can demand using my notebook computer. Via a wireless base station, the other members of my family have the same access to this global electronic library at their computers. For a significant portion of each day, we all spend time at our computers consuming. The products that we are consuming are not made of magnesium, steel, or plastic. They are made of information—an assembly of information raw materials.

We are establishing an amazing capacity for information. Paul Gilster, a columnist and author of the book *Digital Literacy*, recently wrote that "... hard disks will continue to grow in capacity, with 300 gigabyte drives common by year's end" (2003). He continued, "Within two years, new recording technologies will make one terabyte drives standard on desktop PCs ... enough storage for 500 hours of DVD-quality video." A group of scientists at the Stanford Linear Accelerator Center recently transmitted 6.7 gigabytes of information from California to the Netherlands (6,800 miles) in less than a minute (<http://www.slac.stanford.edu/slac/media-info/20030207>).

These astounding increases in capacity beg the questions, "Where will all of this content come from?" or "Will the concept of reruns take on a whole new meaning?" In the future, there will be an enormous demand for information products, and many, if not most, of today's students will be producing these products. They will grow up to be information construction workers, processing, manipulating, and assembling information raw materials into unique and valuable information products. They will utilize a wide variety of digital tools to work with these raw materials, molding them into content that people will value.

If this idea of information-based work is a reasonable speculation, then we need to start looking at education, and the process of teaching and learning, in some different ways. Traditionally, we have considered information to be the end product of the education process; if the student knew this body of information, then he or she was educated. Assuming a rapidly changing and information-driven future, what our children know will be less important than what they can do with it. Rather than being the end product, we must look at information as a raw material that students not only learn, but also use in some way. This is not a difficult task. We only need to think of whom and under what conditions someone would use the information and then simulate such an activity for students. In those few instances that there is no person or profession that would use the information, then perhaps we should not be teaching it. There is more than enough information for students to learn that is useful in the real world.

Employing Text

Text was the preeminent material of information products in the twentieth century, and it will continue to play an important part in the information that we share with each other in the coming decades. For one thing, there is a lot of it out there, and a significant number of people can decode it for meaning. In addition, it takes a fairly low level of technology to share information in text. It can even be printed on paper.

Another benefit of text is the fact that there is a lot of it available to be mined and processed digitally. When I was young and was asked to write a report, I was pretty much limited to two or three sets of encyclopedias and the reference books that were available in our small library. Even with few sources of information, a significant amount of the work that went into my report was spent on rewriting the information that I found, paraphrasing as much as I possibly could, because using someone else's information in his or her words was frowned upon.

In Asia, copying someone else's ideas is considered an expression of respect. This is a sentiment that I believed as I paraphrased intelligent and well-written pieces of information into my clumsy way of explaining things. Of course, I was being taught to write, not copy. However, we must ask the question, "How much will our evolving tools for processing text change the rules of how we assemble our information products?" When furniture was made by hand, it often included artistic embellishments that distinguished one piece from another, one artisan from another. Now that furniture is manufactured in factories where materials are assembled into functional products of value, the styles of these products have become less marked by craftsmanship and more for utility. With the increased digitization of information, I wonder if writing may go the same way and become more an assembly of other people's texts rather than the almost exclusively original and crafted text that was expected from me. Just as there remain artisans who continue to craft furniture to be works of beauty, we will continue to have writers who are able to affect us on many levels with the beauty of their words. For the rest of us, communicating our ideas and accomplishing our goals will be why we write, and if somebody else has said it better, why not borrow or purchase those words?

Before you haul this author up and burn him in effigy, there are certainly ethical issues, not to mention laws, that are designed to protect people's intellectual properties, and it is not the intent of this chapter to suggest that we circumvent those laws or courtesies. It is a logical speculation that because our information processing tools seem designed to pick up well-expressed ideas and place them in other settings, this practice may become an accepted way of creating information products.

Think of the building of walls in ancient times. To conserve energy, people frequently took the bricks from old walls and assembled them into new ones with specific goals in mind. A new wall was being built in order to keep something or someone in, or to keep them out. It really did not matter who produced the original bricks, because the true strength of the wall depended on the order of the bricks and to an even greater degree on the mortar that held them together.

If the assignment is to produce an information product for a real audience and a specific goal for affecting that audience, then the task is to identify blocks of information that are relevant to the assignment, and to assemble them in a way that accomplishes the goal. Empowering those blocks of ideas to deliver the message in a consistent and clear way requires carefully sequencing the ideas and binding them with mortar that holds them together, creating a context, and delivering smooth and effective communication. The student's task is to mine the network (and other sources) for valuable information blocks, assemble them into a logical order, and bind them together by applying their own text between the blocks. As a result, students are spending more time finding, evaluating, and making meaning from existing information and less time working in the technique and craft of writing.

The suggestion here is that we concentrate more on students delivering a consistent, logical, and valuable product, and less on the amount of writing that they accomplish in the process, recognizing that writing remains an essential part of these communications. It is also important to state here, even though ethics and information will be covered extensively in a later chapter, that information is property, and that other people's property must be respected appropriately. Students must learn to credit the ideas of others as they expect their ideas to be credited. It is difficult to predict how new information processing tools and immediate access to a global library of digital content will affect writing, but it is safe to say that those effects will be determined by the people who are currently in our classrooms.

Writing aside, there are a variety of ways that digital text can be employed for teaching and for learning. For instance, one of the unique qualities of networked digital text is that it can be indexed and searched. For instance, I recently wrote an article about electronic ink, or E-Ink (go to this book's Web site to learn more about E-Ink). I happened to remember that Jeffery Harrow, a writer on the topic of emerging technologies, had covered electronic ink in a number of issues of his online newsletter "Rapidly Changing Face of Computing". I was able to employ the digital nature of his text to access and use those ideas by searching with Google for: *E-Ink site:www.compaq.com*.

As we learned in the previous chapter, this search phrase asked for all Web pages that include the term "E-Ink" within the Web domain "www.compaq.com", the home of Harrow's online newsletter. This is not an insignificant accomplishment considering that that only 25 letters and symbols successfully located the three or four pertinent articles from the billions of Web pages on the Internet.

As another example, we can ask students to teach themselves about U.S. history by giving them a word processing file that includes all of the inaugural addresses of all the presidents of the United States. Such a file can be created from the following Web site: <http://www.landmark-project.com/Inaugural_addresses.html>.

Load the page, highlight the text, copy it, and paste it into a word processing file, and then put the file on the network so that students can access it through computers in their classroom or computer lab. Students can then employ this information by searching for keywords related to their studies, easily finding each time that a president uttered those words, and learning about the context of the words' meaning during that decade.

A more striking way that digital information can be employed is the use of tabular data. The Internet holds an enormous amount of data that is published by universities, research centers, and the government and covers an astounding range of topics. Data can be found that describes the weather, air quality, sports, labor, geography, demographics, crime, biology, economics, and many other subjects. One of my favorites is the Advanced National Seismic System (ANSS). Its Web site provides an online catalog (database) of seismic events, a composite of several other catalogs maintained by various agencies and organizations. The ANSS database is searchable so that I can identify the types of earthquakes I want to learn about and it will generate a data set on those quakes. For instance, when I go to the **ANSS Catalog Search** page (<http://quake.geo.berkeley.edu/anss/catalog-search.html>) and indicate, using a Web form, that I want to see all seismic events beginning *2003/01/01,00:00:00* and ending *2003/02/01,00:00:00* (quakes during the month of January 2003) at least 3.0 in magnitude on the Richter scale, it generates 14 pages of data on individual quakes from around the world. The data includes the date and time of the event, its latitude and longitude, the magnitude, depth at the epicenter, and additional information that I do not understand.

Using the mouse, I can highlight the entire data set, copy it into the computer's clipboard, and then paste the data directly into an empty Microsoft Excel spreadsheet. Unfortunately, the entire table of data flows into only the first column of the spreadsheet, but we can spread the data out and format it for the spreadsheet by highlighting that first column, pulling down the **Data** menu, and selecting **Text to Columns**. A series of wizards appear, each asking how the information is to be formatted.

In the first wizard (figure 3.1), you are asked to determine how the columns should be identified or delimited. If, in the preview box toward the bottom of the window, the columns seem to line up, then select **Fixed Width**. If they do not, then select **Delimited**. Delimited means that there is a character, usually a tab or a comma, between the items that separates the columns.

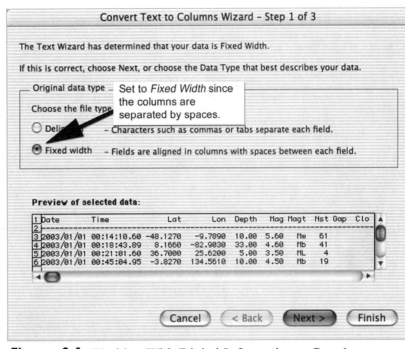

Figure 3.1: Working With Digital Information—Part 1

If you selected **Fixed Width**, then you will have an opportunity in the next wizard window (figure 3.2) to move the column breaks around and even add new ones, or delete existing ones.

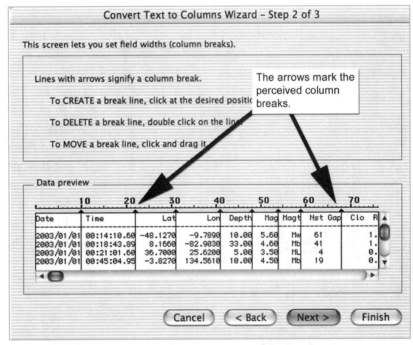

Figure 3.2: Working With Digital Information—Part 2

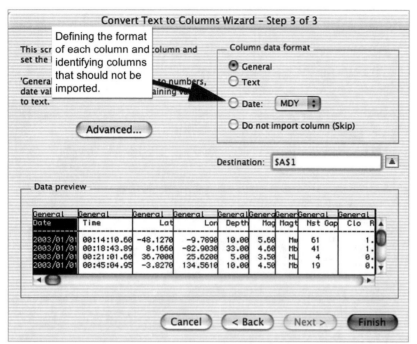

Figure 3.3: Working With Digital Information — Part 3

In the next wizard window (figure 3.3), you can select each column and determine how the information should be formatted. Selecting **General** will treat the information in this column as a value that can be calculated in a formula. This is for columns that are exclusively numbers. Columns that hold text would be marked as **Text**. If the column contains a date or time, then selecting **Date** will have the information formatted in the date/time layout of your choosing. Finally, if there is a column that is not necessary for your purposes, then click the **Do not import column (Skip)** radio button, and it will not be included in the resulting spreadsheet.

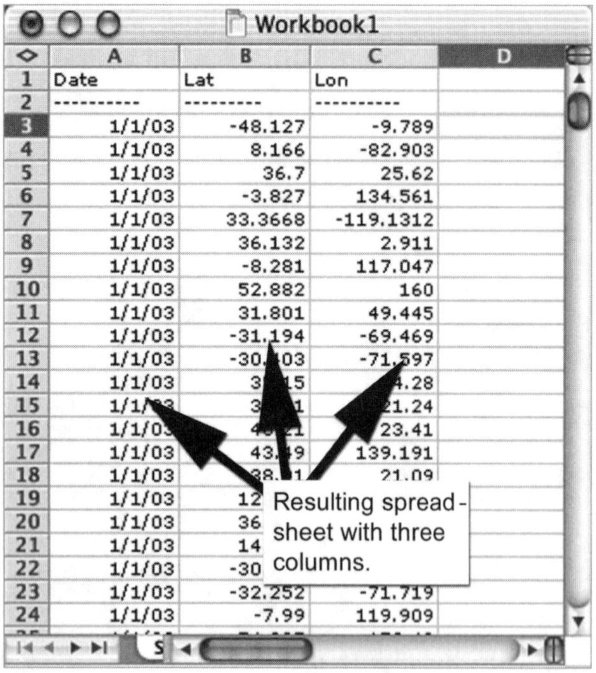

Figure 3.4: Working With Digital Information — Part 4

When you click the **Finish** button, the pasted information is converted into a spreadsheet (figure 3.4). In my example of the earthquake data, I import only the *date, latitude,* and *longitude* of each seismic event. In case you are following along with your own experiment, it is important that the latitude data be to the right of the longitude data. To accomplish this, highlight the latitude column and cut it. Then highlight the column to the right of the longitude and paste. To cause this data to actually tell me something, I highlight the block of data, the longitude and latitude, and click the graphing tool icon.

There is much that you can do to label and format a graph. I simply select the **Scatter Plot** graph and then click finish. The resulting graph marks X/Y coordinates to the longitude/latitude values of the earthquakes (figure 3.5). The horizontal zero (0) line represents the Equator, while the vertical zero (0) line represents the Prime Meridian. The dots generated by the plot represent individual seismic events of at least 3.0 on the Richter scale and occurring during the month of January 2003. The result is a rather dramatic representation of the planet's tectonic plates, the ring of fire around the Pacific Rim, and so on. Text data is helping us to see. It tells a story.

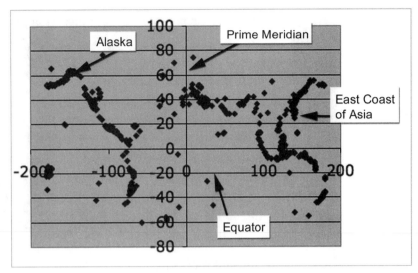

Figure 3.5: Working With Digital Information — Part 5

Processing digital text is a practice that many of us take for granted today. It is a part of twenty-first century literacy that seems un-extraordinary any more. However, it is important, as we continue to exist and prosper in a rapidly changing and increasingly information-driven world, to remember that digital information is made to be manipulated. This is its best feature. We can process, change, attach and detach, convert, translate, and rewrite information in powerful and compelling ways, and for those who continue to think about this, the possibilities will continue to grow.

Employing Images

Today, nearly every classroom has access to a digital camera. Many classrooms have their own camera that is used nearly every day. According to the technology intelligence and analysis firm, IDC, more than 10 million digital cameras were sold in 2002. There are lots of reasons why people are purchasing cameras that connect to their computers, but the most important reason is that the picture taking is only the first step in the process of picture making.

The fundamental difference between digital pictures and the traditional chemically processed variety is the fact that each dot in the picture (pixel) is represented by a number or a series of numbers. Computers love numbers and can alter them in an instant. When managing large quantities of related numbers, the computer can produce some fascinating results.

The picture represented in figure 3.6 on the following page was taken during a recent trip to Southport, North Carolina. The only processing that has been done to both versions of the picture in the figure is deleting all colors, converting it to grayscale for the sake of publishing.

The effect of the second version of the picture was accomplished by loading the picture into an image processing program and applying a filter called Palette Knife. The filter is a set of programs that sifts through all of the numbers involved in defining each pixel (individual dot in the picture). In the case of the Palette Knife, the filter takes pixels that are

Before   After

Figure 3.6: Image Processing

in the same general location and have similar values, averages their values, and then applies the processed values back to the pixels. The effect is a picture that looks as though it were painted in oil or acrylic with a palette knife.

  The image processing software that has become synonymous with this type of operation is PhotoShop from Adobe Systems. However, to use this powerful and highly flexible tool requires some knowledge about graphic art and a considerable amount of time to learn it. In addition, PhotoShop is prohibitively expensive for most schools. As an alternative, Adobe has recently released a less sophisticated version called PhotoShop Elements. It is a scaled-down version of the professional product and costs less than $100. I have used both products and found that there is little I was doing with PhotoShop that I cannot do with Elements.

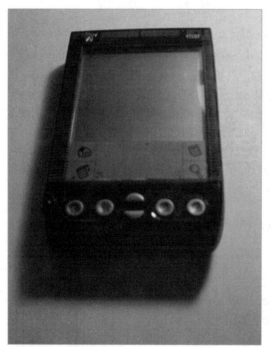

  There are a number of other useful image processing packages that involve a relatively shallow learning curve, but offer useful processing features. Among them are Paint Shop Pro for Windows and GraphicConverter for the Mac OS.

  One of the most useful features of many of these programs is layering. With layering, you can have many different pictures stacked on top of each other so that individual components or layers can be altered independently. For an example, look at the picture in figure 3.7 of a Handspring Visor PDA.

  For a teacher who is going to start using a set of hand-held computing devices, it would be wise to produce a document that describes to students how to use these tools. In this case, a photograph is taken with a digital camera, loaded to a computer, and opened into PhotoShop Elements.

Figure 3.7: Image Layers — Part 1

A new layer is created on which information can be painted, pasted, or typed without affecting the original photograph. On this layer, *On/Off Switch* is typed (See figure 3.8).

To better highlight the text, a new layer is added between the text layer and the original picture. On this layer, a white rectangle is created to go behind the text (See figure 3.9).

In the third evolution of this picture (figure 3.10), the layer with the rectangle is set to produce a shadow to better distinguish this information from the original image. A new layer is also created with a line and arrow. That layer is moved so that the beginning of the line rests behind the rectangle.

One of the most impressive examples of student work using digital information is a movie created by Mr. Spencer Reisinger's elementary class at Barrett Elementary School in Arlington, Virginia. His students used pencil and colors to draw the sets and characters of *Molly Bannaky*, a children's book by Alice McGill. The images were then digitized using a flat scanner and arranged in layers using Photoshop, with the help of the school's technology facilitator, Ms. Shaw. In layers, the students could move the characters around over the scene, creating individual pictures that could then be imported into iMovie, a video editing program that comes pre-installed on all Macintosh computers. The pictures were then arranged as a video and sequenced to tell the story, with each image set to display for a specific number of seconds. You can see their work at <http://www.arlington.k12.va.us/schools/barrett/molly>.

Employing Audio

In 1986, 20th Century Fox produced and distributed a movie that spawned three sequels (a fourth is currently in production), two TV series, and one animated series. There was little about the movie, *Highlander*, that would indicate its future success. The story involves a race of sword-wielding immortals who travel through the centuries surviving by lopping off the heads of other immortals and trying not to lose their own. Performances by European-born Christopher Lambert and an aging and stiff Sean Connery had less to do with the success of this movie than the soundtrack and the superb editing that tied together vision and music.

The seductively dark atmosphere was in large measure enhanced by the lush music composed and performed by John Deacon, Brian May, Roger Taylor, and

Figure 3.8: Image Layers —Part 2

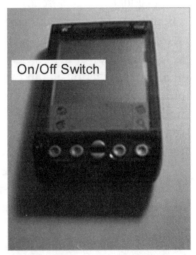

Figure 3.9: Image Layers —Part 3

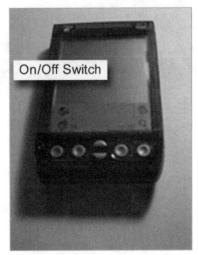

Figure 3.10: Image Layers —Part 4

Freddie Mercury of the '80s rock band Queen. The cinematography of the Scottish Highlands and the highly synthesized music combined to create a movie experience that was difficult to see only once. I have watched the movie at least 10 times.

We tend not to depend on only one sense as we experience the world around us. Though most of us identify more with sight than we do with the other senses, what we hear, smell, touch, and taste are each essential in defining our reality—and communication is merely one person's attempt at sharing aspects of his or her reality with others.

There is a student-produced video that I frequently show at conferences. The visual aspects, by themselves, are not especially impressive. In fact, the video consists mostly of still images and text messages that float or shake across the screen, but the background audio, the hauntingly beautiful *Sacrifice* by Lisa Gerrard and Pieter Bourke, turns the communication into an emotional experience. Music communicates to many of us in a way that even the most well-crafted words will not. It can turn our emotions—and where the emotions go, the mind and body follow.

There is a problem, though, with integrating music into student-produced information products. It has already been suggested in this chapter that students should be free to assemble independent information materials into a unique and valuable information product. As stated before, this should only be done with proper respect and credit to the owners and strict adherence to the law. Our problem is that getting permission to use copyrighted information from the music (and video) industry is probably more difficult to achieve than any other source. In fact, impossible is probably a more accurate word. Several years ago I got in the habit of playing Glenn Miller's *In the Mood*, as audiences entered the hall I was presenting in. It was especially good for sessions after lunch, because making teachers tap their feet helped to keep them awake.

One day, in the middle of a presentation on copyright, a teacher asked me how I went about getting permission to play Glenn Miller before the session began. I was stumped and stopped dead in my tracks; I have not played anyone else's music to a paying audience since. However, this gave me an opportunity to pursue an interest I had had for some time. I invested in a synthesizer, a musical keyboard that can synthesize or imitate a variety of existing instruments and even new sounds that have never been produced by traditional musical instruments. The keyboard that I purchased (figure 3.11), as do most synthesizers, has MIDI capabilities.

MIDI (Musical Instrument Digital Interface) means that the keyboard can exchange information with a computer. As notes are played on the keyboard, the corresponding data that describes each note (pitch, tone, instrument, duration, and so on) is sent to the computer, where software (figure 3.12) stores it for later processing. Data can also be sent to the keyboard, causing it to play the music that is stored and encoded by the computer into a digital message.

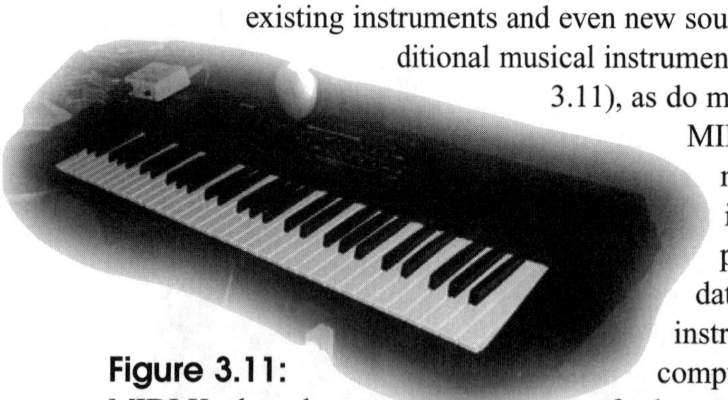

Figure 3.11:
MIDI Keyboard

I play around with the keyboard, playing notes until I hear a combination that is pleasing to me. Then, having connected the keyboard to my computer and launched a piece of software that will communicate with the keyboard, I play the notes again, while the software captures each note, its duration, tonal qualities, and volume and records the information. The recorded music can then be displayed on the computer as a musical score, or in a simple grid for those of us who cannot interpret musical notation.

When the musical data is contained within the computer and displayed in an understandable fashion on the screen, it is ready to be employed. Various aspects of the individual notes can be altered, changing the nature of the music and the quality of the song. Notes can be dragged

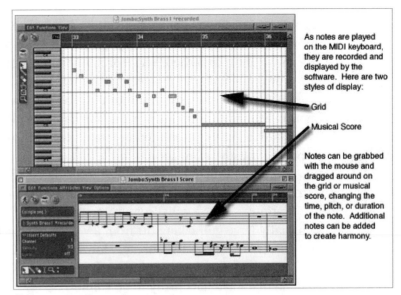

As notes are played on the MIDI keyboard, they are recorded and displayed by the software. Here are two styles of display:

• Grid

• Musical Score

Notes can be grabbed with the mouse and dragged around on the grid or musical score, changing the time, pitch, or duration of the note. Additional notes can be added to create harmony.

Figure 3.12: MIDI Software Grid

from place to place on the grid, changing their pitch and when they are played. Notes and sequences of notes can be copied and pasted again, replicating their play. Notes can even be stretched out and contracted, changing the duration of their play. The benefit to us, as educators and learners, is that we can compose and perform our own music without years of study and practice in mastering a musical instrument.

To make things even more interesting, we can add additional note sets assigning different instruments. These are called tracks. We are stacking one instrument and its music on top of other instruments, resulting in an entire band. The keyboard that I purchased can perform 16 different voices at the same time—a small orchestra, considering that one voice, strings for instance, can sound like multiple musicians.

Accomplishing the composition and editing with a computer mouse makes musical communication accessible to many more people than would have the opportunity in a world of only pianos and horns. This does not mean that we will forget about traditional instruments or that fewer people will play them. My son spends hours a day perfecting his technique in playing the baritone and hopes to major in music when he enters college. Playing this one instrument well is his passion. Mine is constructing an entire musical experience in my spare time with computer and mouse. In the twenty-first century, we can do either and both because we can employ the information.

Employing Video

I will spend quite a few pages on video production in the next chapter. It is a tool for communicating, but I want to suggest here that we think about video cameras in a different way. Video has been around for many years. For most of that time sophisticated movie cameras and editing technologies have been exclusively available to highly trained professionals in the entertainment and news industries. Today, however, with quality digital cameras available for less than $500 and powerful editing software pre-installed on many computers, the potentials of these technologies are significantly expanding. Our tendency, though, is to think about video capabilities, as educators, in traditional terms. As a result, we have established studios in our media centers and have begun offering news programming performed and managed by students, sports event playbacks, and other applications of video to which we are accustomed. These are not bad uses of these tools, but we should realize that the growing ubiquity of this technology will redefine how it is used.

Think about your school or classroom digital video camera as an input device, like a mouse, keyboard, or scanner. It is a machine that allows us to capture information about the world around us and then input it into a computer, where we can manipulate, enhance, and experiment with information.

As an example, a number of years ago, I shot some video while taking a walk through a neighborhood park. The lake, around which the park is situated, had become a winter refuge for sea gulls from the coast. During this walk, I captured on digital tape an especially large gull taking off from a wooden bridge and flying across the lake. The grace of this animal was overwhelming. However, when I imported the video into my computer, loading it into iMovie, a free videoediting program preinstalled on all Macintosh computers, I found that I had data ready to be employed.

One of the features of iMovie is the drag ball that can be moved to the left, toward the icon of a turtle, or to the right, toward a rabbit. The effect is to make the video play more slowly or faster. The effect of viewing the bird flying in slow motion was magnificent. It was visually breathtaking but also educational. I was able to show my students the nuances of how a bird flies: the angles of its wings, how its joints work, the shape of its wings, the cycle rate, and more. I might also set the camera on a tripod and video a blooming flower or a tray of grass leaning toward light on the right, and then leaning back to a new light source on the left. After the video has been imported into the video editor, it can be sped up to dramatically illustrate motion in the plant world. Because motion can be captured and then edited, we can employ that information to reveal what was initially invisible to the human eye. We are able to enhance our knowledge by employing the information.

Conclusion

In the twentieth century, we were taught by math teachers to work with information. In most other classes under most circumstances, we simply learned information. In the twenty-first century, we will all be working with information; not all of that information will be numbers, but almost all of it will be digital. For this reason, we must start changing our notions about the skills that we teach, especially those that we typically include in the math curriculum. Being able to count, measure, calculate, and manipulate numbers will remain a prerequisite for being literate in the twenty-first century. However, students must be learning to do these things with digital information in order to accomplish goals. They must learn the skills involved in employing information.

Action Items

Directors of Technology

■ Emphasize the use of productivity tools in your technology program (word processing, spreadsheets, databases, graphics, music, and video production). Offer professional development accordingly.

- Establish an annual technology fair for your district. Establish booths where teachers and students demonstrate their digital work and discuss what they learn and teach in the process.
- Establish a district mailing list for teachers to use in discussing how they are employing digital information.
- Create a district museum of student- and teacher-constructed information products organized by subject area. This can be a video exhibit at the district office or a Web site.

Principals

- When delivering performance and demographic data to teachers for use in planning, demonstrate how the data is employed to tell a story about your school and its strengths, weaknesses, and other characteristics.
- During evaluations, ask teachers how they are using digital information to teach. Are they manipulating the information in any way? Also ask what students are doing with digital information to construct new knowledge.
- Purchase digital still and video cameras so that any teacher can make use of the technology at any time. Work toward providing a still and video camera for each classroom.
- Ask to see student-produced digital products (reports on disk, Web pages, multimedia presentations, software).
- Establish a section of the school's Web site for showcasing student and teacher productions.

Media Specialists

- Establish a digital library of student-produced digital products: reports, Web pages, images, tunes, and video. Make these products available to other students as information raw materials for future work.
- Make sure that computer work stations in your media center give students access to productivity tools (word processing, spreadsheets, graphics, music, and video production), as well as staff to support students in their use of the tools.
- Set up one or more computers in the media center as a display station for showcasing digital products created by students or teachers.
- Establish a section of the media center Web site to showcase student productions.

School Tech Facilitators

- Map the school's curriculum in a way that you and the media specialist have access to what is currently being taught by each teacher. Use this information to suggest ways for teachers and students to employ digital information for teaching and learning.
- Offer ongoing professional development in the use of productivity software for creating digital products. Maintain a digital library of teacher-constructed digital files and make the library available to all teachers.

- Explore ways that scientists, engineers, and business people employ information in their work. Look closely at scientific computation, using computers to visualize large amounts of data.

Teachers

- Take every opportunity to play with your computer. Play around with spreadsheets. Take some pictures and load them into a graphics program and just start clicking buttons to see what the effects are.
- Identify the students in your classroom who are already adept at using productivity software. Ask for their advice on an ongoing basis, even if the information is not digital (Terri, what could we do with this information if we found it on the Internet?).
- Think of the computer as a laboratory. Create a spreadsheet with demographic information or scientific observations, and ask students to learn something from it. Use your class experts as consultants.
- Note those students who do not have easy access to technology outside of the classroom and explore ways of getting it to them through the school tech facilitator, media specialist, principal, district offices, and community leaders.

Students

- Play with your computers. I know that this is like telling a fish to swim, but take advantage of the time you have. It is your only advantage over us.
- Suggest extra-credit assignments that you can perform by analyzing or manipulating data.
- If you do not understand a concept, a process, or another piece of knowledge, ask your teacher if you can see a picture, or a video, or a diagram.

Parents

- Make sure that each of your children has access to a computer that is connected to the Internet. This does not mean that each child should have his or her own computer, but that each child has access.
- Install productivity software on your home computer(s). This would include word processing, spreadsheets, graphics software, and music and video production. Especially cater to special interests of your children (art, music, photography, writing, and so on).
- If your job involves employing information in some way, explain it to your children. If possible, take them to your workplace and demonstrate. Explain what you have to know and the experience you need in order to perform this task.

4 Expressing Ideas Compellingly

When I was young, I played little league baseball. I was not very good at it until my last year when I developed enough strength and coordination to be useful to the team. I understood, though, that the most glamorous position on the baseball team was the pitcher. Even though being a catcher was also cool, because of the gear you wore, the pitcher was the one player whom everyone watched on every play.

His job was to use velocity and spin to alter the angle of trajectory, and a certain amount of psychology, to get the ball past the batter. If the batter saw through the psychology and was able to compensate for the angle and match the velocity, then he connected with the ball and stood a chance of being the hero.

Baseball was not a sport of choice for my children. They played soccer and participated on the swim team. Today, more often than not, when someone talks about pitching, it has to do with pitching an idea, or convincing someone to accept your vision. The pitcher still uses velocity, spin, and psychology to make the pitch, but the goal is to help the receiver connect, not to get the idea past them. As more of the manufacturing of our products are automated, people will spend their time dealing with the information that drives that production: inventory planning, marketing, and the systems that provide the structure for supporting it all. Success and prosperity will depend less on natural resources and more on the development and crafting of that information system—and the communication that happens within it. Systems will compete with other systems, and success will depend on the quality of the information and how it is presented.

Our personal shopping is increasingly based on information. We shop from home, in front of a computer, browsing through Web sites, comparing information—not products. In the Information Age, information will compete for attention in much the same way that products on a store shelf competed for attention during the Industrial Age.

One of the most important reasons that we communicate is to affect the behavior of other people. You want someone to have a higher regard for you. You may want someone to pick your plan for improvement over that of a competitor or colleague. You may want to affect the voting behavior of constituents, homework habits of your students, or buying habits of consumers. These are all accomplished by expressing ideas clearly and compellingly.

This is old news for educators. Our job is to sell ideas and to affect what students know, believe, and can do. We do this not by simply delivering content, but by creating and crafting messages that cause students to gain the knowledge that is required. In recent years, we have learned more about how people think and learn. As a result, we have improved our techniques for helping our students gain knowledge and skills by delivering messages in a

Large Idea!

In the Information Age, information will compete for attention in much the same way that products on a store shelf competed for attention in the Industrial Age.

Instant Messaging Grammar

Participating in an Instant Messaging conversation (IM'ing) requires agreed upon conventions in order to communicate effectively and efficiently. Two rules seem to underlie IM communication. One is that capital letters serve to increase the auditory volume of the conversation. In other words, you capitalize in order to shout, and this is considered rude in most circumstances. So all text is generally in lower case. Shift keys also slow you down.

Secondly, IM'ers do not use punctuation, except for commas, which they find to be indispensable. Again, extra keys slow you down and they are all in difficult to reach positions.

IM'ing makes extensive use of abbreviations and a series of punctuations to simulate facial expressions, emoting gestures of emotion.

Abb.	Explanation
:-)	Happy face
;-)	Winking happy face
:-(	Sad face
^_^	Happy anime face
bbl	Be Back Later
bc	BeCause
brb	Be Right Back
btw	By The Way
grrrr	Growl, expression of anger
hw	HomeWork
im	Instant Messenger
jk	Just Kidding
K	oK!
lmao	Laugh My Ass Off
lol	Laughing Out Loud
nmh	Not Much Here
nmu	Not Much, yoU?
o	Oh
omg	Oh My Gosh (form of exclamation)
r	aRe
sn	Screen Name
sp	previous word may be misSPelled
sup	what'S UP?
thankz	thank you
ttfn	Ta Ta For Now!
ttyl	Talk To You Later
u	yoU
ur	yoUR/you're

Figure 4.1: Instant Messaging Grammar (Warlick)

variety of ways. This is a realization that we should impart to our students because they will all become teachers, and for that they will need powerful communication skills.

Communicating Compellingly — Text

Traditionally, we have taught writing as the communication skill. We have helped students to learn the rules of grammar and syntax, punctuation, and spelling. Many of us have even helped students learn to be good writers, able to influence and entertain other people with their words. This will not end. As the director Martin Scorcese says, "… whatever cinema evolves into, you will still need an author."

It is important, as we reflect on the technological changes in communication, that we think about the effects that these new tools may have on the quality of writing. I recently attended a meeting of educators who were discussing technology in the classroom. The suggestion arose that we allow students to use instant messaging software in the classroom in order to conduct collaborative and cooperative learning activities. One teacher immediately asked, "How do we assure that the students will be practicing good writing while they are messaging instead of using all of those short cuts?" Other educators in the room nodded their heads in agreement, and the idea was dropped.

What these and many other educators fail to understand is that these children have invented a new grammar specifically designed for a communication avenue that is unique to their generation. We should respect this and even marvel at how well these kids have adapted a new tool to their tasks and lifestyle and to enriching their personal relationships. Their new grammar is not intended to replace the old, but to serve a unique purpose. At the same time that we teach them the grammar of formal writing, we should be willing to ask them to teach us their new grammar for synchronous writing (See figure 4.1).

Traditionally, we have taught writing through avenues that are fairly artificial and specific to the academic arena. We have asked students to write essays, themes, and research papers. The fact is that outside of our classrooms, people rarely write essays, themes, or research papers. We write letters, reports, e-mail messages, and persuasive copy that are aimed at influencing other people.

To teach students to write compellingly, we must give them compelling reasons to write. Students should produce authentic information products, aimed at real audiences, with meaningful goals in mind. This is not as difficult as it might seem. There are models out there, though not in the arena of writing instruction.

When I was in high school, I took a number of vocational education classes. They included industrial arts, drafting, and a number of clerical courses. Where I lived in the 1960s, the skills taught in these classes were highly relevant considering the focus on manufacturing and the fact that most high-school graduates would be seeking employment in the local mills and factories after graduation. The assignments that came out of those classes were different in nature from those that I received in my academic classes. They involved the design or construction of products that people might actually use. There was an authentic audience and authentic goal for the work. The teacher did not simply deliver content, but served as a consultant or facilitator, helping us to ask the right questions, and to make decisions regarding technique, materials, and tools. In the Information Age, it makes perfect sense to model instruction of information skills after the vocational instruction techniques of the Industrial Age.

Devising authentic assignments is different from traditional ones, but it is not difficult. See figure 4.2 for steps in crafting authentic writing assignments.

Inventing an Authentic Assignment

Task	Example
1. Who, in the adult world, would pay attention to this topic?	Geography is the topic. One profession that would be interested in this topic is travel agents.
2. What kind of information product might this person create or use?	The travel agent would use and, in many cases, create travel brochures.
3. What would be the goal of the information product?	The goal of the travel brochure would be to convince people that they should travel to a specific place.
4. What specific information and format/media would be required to accomplish the goal?	Geographic and culture facts, pictures, video clips, quotes from people who have been there or who live there.

Assignment: Ask students to work in teams to produce a travel brochure to New Zealand and include in the evaluation rubric a provision that determines the persuasiveness of the product.

Figure 4.2: Authentic Assignments

When we shop online, we are comparing information; we are not comparing the actual products. In order to effectively compete for attention, information must communicate itself as efficiently as possible. This is a concept that we have come to realize with the advent of the World Wide Web. For the earliest Web publishers (myself included), Web development was largely a technical endeavor. You learned HTML (HyperText Markup Language) in order to create hyperlinks between documents and to accomplish some basic formatting of the information. Hyperlinks, not formatting, were the great benefit of the Web—the ability to connect similar and supporting documents together—creating a web of information. As new features like tables, animated GIFs, and frames became available, they were considered enhancements that we used to demonstrate our technical prowess. Unfortunately, these formatting enhancements frequently rendered our information useless as they distracted attention away from the message rather than improve it.

As we started using our Web log files (statistics on Web usage) and saw that an enormous and growing number of people were actually looking at our pages, we began to wonder what the viewers of our pages were actually doing with the information, how these visits were helping them, and how they were helping us. Thus, we began to pay more attention to how the information communicated itself. We began to tone down the frames and animated GIFs, and to hide our use of tables for information layout. We also began to look at Web publishing as a way to accomplish our goals by influencing other people. We began to communicate.

If information is competing for attention, then we must learn to package the information in much the same way that we package products for the store shelf. While we fill our pages with pictures and paragraphs of coherent and compelling text, we must consider the various levels in which people access information. For instance, what do people learn from a document upon first glance? Usually, when people consider a document, they have some of the following questions in mind:

- How much time will I invest in this document?
- Will it hold the solution to my question or problem?
- How much am I going to have to work, intellectually, to understand this information?
- Will I be better off after reading this information than I was before?

Information that successfully competes for attention will help readers to start answering these questions before they even start to read.

Figure 4.3 lists a few rules that you might consider when developing a report, project description, handout, worksheet, or when evaluating your students' information products.

Regardless of whether students are producing a written report or a Web page, picture, multimedia presentation, or software, communication needs to become a core part of its evaluation. Consider including at least one element in your evaluation rubrics that asks how well the student has arranged the information for communication. It might read like figure 4.4 on page 68.

Less Is Better	After writing your text, go back and identify every word or phrase that does not help you deliver your message or accomplish your goal. Then delete it. You will find that you can lose as much as half of your text when you do this.
Short Paragraphs	Presenting text in six short paragraphs, with white space between, looks like less reading than presenting two or three long paragraphs. Try to keep paragraphs down to three or four sentences each.
Hanging Indents	Headings and subheadings should be flush to the left of the page margin. The content should be indented. The hanging headings make the document easier to scan.
Bold Important Words and Phrases	Select words and phrases that will be of special interest to the reader or that help you draw attention to the information you want to be read. Bold these words to create eye magnets so that the scanning reader will easily find them.
Bulleted Lists	Any list of two or more items should be bulleted. A bulleted or numbered list is easier to read, study, and learn. A list is a specific type of information, and it should be distinguished from prose.
Use Font & Style Changes	Your document may include several types of information, such as: descriptions, instructions, captions, or lists. These various types of information are read in different ways. It should be clear to the reader, at a glance, when information type has changed. One way to do this is by changing the text's font, size, indention, or style.
Use Appropriate Media	Many concepts can be more easily expressed and understood as graphical images, such as graphs, tables, or diagrams. If a concept can be expressed as a graphic organizer, it usually communicates better that way.

Traditional Text

Packaged Text *

* Because of time constraints at the point of its publication, this book follows a more traditional look and feel for this type of professional resource. See Appendix C for a more detailed sample of information layout.

Figure 4.3: Packaging Information

Objective	Below Standard	Standard	Above Standard
Student is attentive to information design to improve communication.	No evidence that the author has considered information layout to improve communication.	Some elements of the document illustrate conscious decisions on the arrangement of information to improve its communication.	The document illustrates consistent and persistent attention to information layout to improve communication.

Figure 4.4: Communication Rubric

In addition, if the assignment has an authentic audience, there may be a way to establish authentic assessment. Several years ago, the Landmark Project ran an online project called Eco-Entrepreneur. Classes on the Internet were asked to form teams of students into mock companies. Each company devised an imaginative new product that it believed people around their age would buy. The companies had to develop the concept of their products so that they could write a sales pitch that was designed to make other people want to purchase the products. After the sales pitches were written, they were uploaded to a Web site where the text became part of a mock online catalog. Then the participating classes were asked to visit the online catalog and select the items they would buy with a specified amount of money on hand. These mock orders were recorded on the site where the writers monitored how many orders they were receiving.

The primary instructional objective of the activity was to help students develop persuasive writing skills. The students evaluated their own work by watching the orders. The more clear, easy to understand, and persuasive their writing, the more orders they received. If teams found that their products were not being ordered, they could refine their sales pitches, re-install them, and continue to watch for orders.

Communicating Compellingly — Images

When packaging information that competes for attention, it is important to decide what kind of voice will best communicate the message. Often, this will be text. Words communicate clearly and can evoke imagination and passion. However, information can frequently communicate itself more fully and clearly with images. For instance, if students are assigned to create a field trip brochure to be used to introduce next year's class to the trip, even the most talented writers will not be able to portray the image of that museum, historic park, or municipal institution as well as a vivid and descriptive picture. This is one reason why every classroom should have access to digital still cameras. Pictures communicate rich information that can be easily grasped by the reader. Images are a language that all brains are wired to understand. Yet, creating a picture that communicates requires skill no less intricate or essential than learning to write.

When students take a picture with a digital camera or produce an image with a graphics program or colored pencil, they should be encouraged to use the picture to deliver a message or to tell a story. Students should be asking the question, "What do I want to accomplish with this picture?"

One way to help students learn to think about pictures as a communication device is to have them try to tell the stories of pictures they encounter around them. As an example, you might take a photograph or painting from a historic event that students are studying. Ask students to list what they see in the picture. They will list the obvious items of the picture. Next, divide the picture vertically and horizontally, into four quadrants, and then ask teams of students to identify what they see in only one quadrant. Here they will see things that were not apparent when looking at the whole picture. Ask the teams to list both physical items and actions that they see in the picture quadrants. The story of the picture will manifest itself in more detail. Finally, ask students how the less obvious elements they see contribute to the overall story or message. Giving students this kind of image reading (literacy) practice will help them to think about the pictures they are producing as avenues of communication.

The National Archives & Records Administration Web site includes many digital sources for pictures and worksheets that will help students learn to read images and other media and, ultimately, how to communicate. The Web site is at <http://www.archives.gov/digital_classroom>.

Think of your classroom digital camera as an everyday tool of expression. Also, think of it as a note-taking tool. Carry it around in your pocket. When you see a student successfully accomplishing an instructional standard, take a picture. Digital cameras are a way of collecting information. If you are giving homework assignments, and routinely write them on the board, take a picture of the board notes every day, and post that picture on the Web. Save yourself some time. If we, as teachers, come to realize the communication power of our images, we can begin to teach it to our students.

Ask students to express what they are learning with pictures. A teacher in North Carolina recently asked students to use their digital cameras to express their vocabulary words with pictures. They used inexpensive Vivitar Vivicam 10 cameras that cost only $44. With this near ubiquitous access to image recording and production technology, students learned to express what they were studying with images, and, as a result, think harder about what they were learning. The teacher reported that the first week that she used this technique, the students made the highest grades of the year on their vocabulary.

We can also build images using graphics software or enhancing photographs to clarify our message. There are a number of software products that are designed to help us communicate with pictures. As mentioned in the last chapter, Adobe Systems' PhotoShop software is the preeminent graphics tool for image editing among professionals. However, for schools, it may be prohibitively expensive. To better serve the image communicator who is not a professional graphic artist, Adobe's scaled down PhotoShop Elements offers the commonly used features of PhotoShop at a fraction of the cost. Figure 4.5 on page 70 lists just a few of the features that are carried over into Photoshop Elements.

In figure 4.6 on page 71, I briefly describe a few of the techniques that I use to communicate with pictures.

Layers	Layers enable you to divide your image into elements that can be manipulated independently and stacked in a variety of ways.
Resizing	Often you need to make your picture larger or smaller. Understand that making a picture larger can result in loss of quality.
Save As (file types)	You can save an image as a variety of file types. TIF and EPS files produce high quality printings. JPG and GIF files work best on the Web.
Tools	Some of the most common and useful tools include: ■ Marquee & Lasso – Enables you to select and capture sections of the image ■ Paint Brush – Enables you to mark your image in a variety of ways by layer ■ Eraser – Will erase sections of your image by layer ■ Text – Allows you to include typed text in your images ■ Shapes – Enable you to add rectangles and circles to your image ■ Eye Dropper – Click a spot on your image, and the color of that spot will be adopted as the default color in your palette ■ Zoom – Usually a magnifying glass icon, this tool enables you to enlarge specific sections of the image for more refined work
Copy & Paste	Elements of an image can be selected (with the marquee or lasso), copied, and pasted onto other images or into specific layers of an image.
Cropping	This enables you to select the most important section of your picture and then remove all outlying sections.

Figure 4.5: Graphic Features

To help them learn to communicate with pictures, ask students to do just that—communicate with each other. Listed below are a few ideas for activities that ask students to communicate with pictures.

1. Give students a list of quotes from literature they are reading. Ask teams (or individuals) to produce a single picture that portrays the idea of the quote. Then ask the entire class to match the pictures with the quotes. If they get it right, the teams did a good job of communicating.
2. After teaching a concept in math, ask students to produce a picture that illustrates how or why the concept might be used outside of the classroom.
3. Ask students to list things that they do every day. Then ask them to produce a set of pictures that will provide instructions on how to perform one of the tasks. Allow the students to include words in their images, but limit the number of words they can use; for instance, "You can include up to 10 words in your picture."
4. If students are studying a historic controversy, or one from current events, ask them to use existing pictures from the Internet to produce a montage that exemplifies one of the positions involved in the controversy.
5. Ask students to take or produce pictures that illustrate the effects of good or bad health habits.

Cropping

Frequently, the picture that you start with has more information on it than you need. Information that does not help you aaccomplish your goal will distract you from your goal. This can often be solved by cropping out the unwanted part of the image. To do this, use the marquee selector to select only the part of the image you want to keep and then select Crop from the Image menu.

Marquee

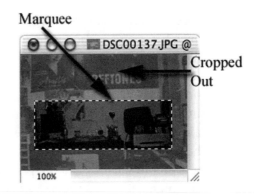

Cropped Out

Clouding

This is another technique for drawing attention to an image. In order to make the focal point of the image part of the document you can use the Eraser tool of the graphics program, set to Air Brush mode, and erase out the surrounding part of the image. This gives a much softer version of the image, making it appear out of the document, rather than stamped onto the page.

Using the eraser to wash out unwanted parts of the image.

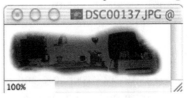

Its appearance within the document

Layering

This is one of the most powerful features of graphics software. In a sense, layering allows you to place a sheet of glass over the picture and then paint on the glass. Anything that you paint on the glass will not affect the original image. The glass or layer can be moved around for position. Additional layers can be added, creating any number of pictures that stack on top of each other and make a single picture.

I frequently add layers to label a picture. In the example to the right, each label is a separate layer allowing it to be positioned to most effectively communicate.

Computer for gaming, research, & music

TV for cable programming & gaming

Handheld Video game

Video game controller

Figure 4.6: Graphics Software

Communicating Compellingly — Animation

Pictures tell stories by standing still. Animation tells a story by moving, showing the difference between one moment and another, a previous condition compared with the result of an independent action. We see animation almost everywhere. It has become an integral part of television communication. Spend a half hour with the nightly news and count the number of times that the program utilizes animation. Watch a five-minute weather report and count. Increasingly, we are seeing animation on flat screen video monitors in stores, elevators, and airports, and at gas pumps. The reason that we are seeing so many animated images is because they communicate. We are a species that is hooked up to time, and comparing one moment to the next is a big part of how we view and understand the world. Once again, communication is a process of helping other people to understand our personal world.

There are four ways of producing animations in the classroom that are relatively practical. The first, and probably least accessible to most schools, is Flash, a product and technology from Macromedia (<http://www.macromedia.com/software/flash/>). This is a sophisticated type of animation that is especially powerful because the user's mouse can interact with the animation, enabling customized actions and even simulations. Flash is not for every teacher, or every school. However, many teachers have learned to use it and some even produce instructional animations for their students. The down side is that Flash authoring is fairly expensive and learning to produce Flash animations requires a fairly steep learning curve for most people.

Another, more accessible form of animation is an animated GIF. A GIF is a type of image file that is frequently used on Web pages. An animated GIF is a single image file that stacks numerous images in layers on top of each other. In a sense, an animated GIF acts like a digital flipbook that plays the individual GIF images in sequence. If each image is a slightly altered version of the previous image, then the effect is motion or animation. For instance, I might use my graphics program to produce an image with the words *Express* and *Yourself*, each in a separate layer. I save the image as file1.gif and then move the two words (layers) a little closer together. Then I save the picture again, this time as file2.gif. I continue this process until I have adjusted and saved the file 10 times (file1.gif to file10.gif). Lined up, they might look like figure 4.7.

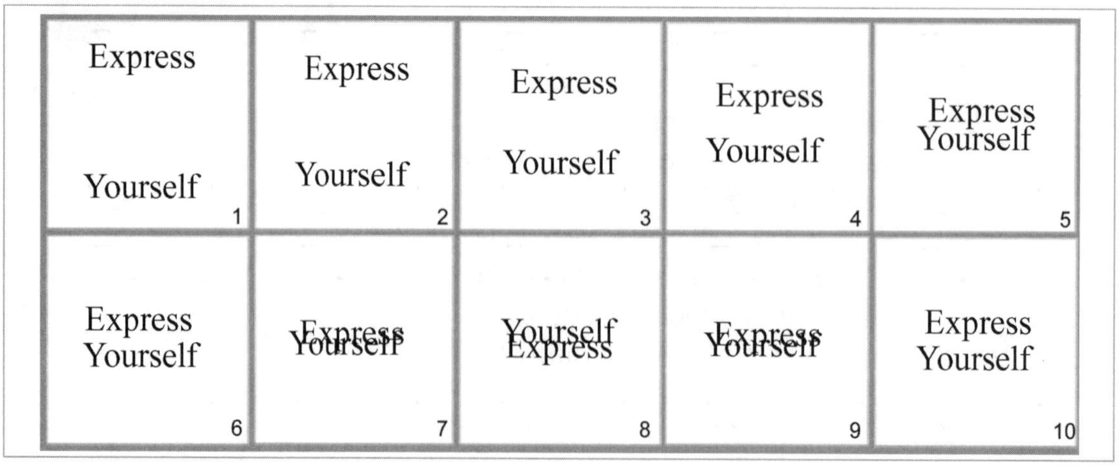

Figure 4.7: Animation 1

I can then run a freeware program, which can be downloaded from the Internet called GifBuilder, and load the 10 individual images into the software. There are a number of parameters that I can set, including how the animation should be looped, transitions between images, and others. I finally save all of the pictures as a single GIF formatted file that will display the animation. You can see the resulting animation at the Web site for this book, <http://landmark-project.com/redefining_literacy/>. Just click the link for this chapter.

Another style of animation that is gaining in popularity, not only in schools, but also among amateur producers, is video animation. The video production done by students at Barrett Elementary School, described in the previous chapter, is an excellent example. Again, you can see the video at <http://www.arlington.k12.va.us/schools/barrett/molly/index.html>.

Many video-editing programs have the ability to import still images and then display them for a prescribed amount of time. The result of importing and playing images with gradually changing elements is animation, and it is a quite accessible form for schools with basic video-editing software.

One of the classic examples of student-produced video is a project called *The Bernoulli Principle*, produced by students at Palmer Junior Middle School. This video, which can be seen at **Apple's Education iMovie Gallery** (<http://www.apple.com/education/dv/gallery>), features five students illustrating experiments that demonstrate the laws of physics and describe how planes fly. Part of the video is a short animation that graphically demonstrates the concept. To produce this animation, the students drew three still images (See figure 4.8).

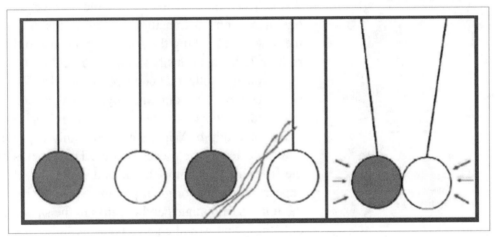

Figure 4.8: Animation 2

Then the pictures were imported into the video-editing software the students were using, Apple's iMovie (<http://www.apple.com/imovie/>), and sequenced between two existing video clips recorded by the team. The effect was a very clear explanation of the concept communicated through animation and voice-over.

A final type of animation, and perhaps the most accessible to students and teachers, is presentation software. Usually not thought of as animation software, presentation tools, such as Microsoft PowerPoint or Hyperstudio, are used routinely by teachers to present content as a high-tech alternative to the chalkboard. PowerPoint and other presentation products are powerful communication tools. They help us pitch our ideas by utilizing text, imagery, sound, and motion. They help us to hit many different senses and styles of learning. If it is taught to students as a communication tool, and students' evaluations are based on the quality of their presentations' content and effectiveness of communication, and not on their technical prowess, then these programs should be an essential part of what and how we teach.

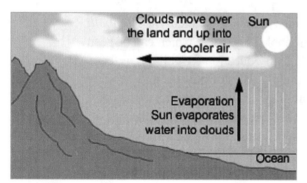

Figure 4.9: Water Cycle — Part 1

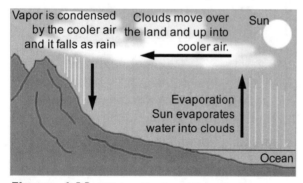

Figure 4.10: Water Cycle — Part 2

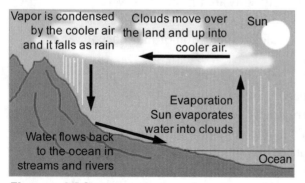

Figure 4.11: Water Cycle — Part 3

Figure 4.12: Water Cycle — Part 4

One example might be to portray the water cycle (See figures 4.9–4.12). We start with a picture of mountains that lead down to the ocean. To build the concept of hydrology, we add to that picture elements that indicate the evaporation of water from the ocean into the air as vapor. Carrying the process through to its next step, we add elements that illustrate how water vapor moves over the mountains and climbs into cooler air where it condenses back into liquid water and falls as rain. Finally, we add a last element indicating how water returns to the ocean through rivers and streams, completing the cycle.

PowerPoint and other presentation programs offer a wide range of transitions that can be employed to move from one slide to another. The tendency among students and teachers is to spend a great deal of time picking the right transition. This is good, as long as this time is invested in selecting the transition that helps communicate the message. For instance, one of the popular transitions is Push. This involves the new slide pushing the preceding one off to the right or left. This transition implies a new slide, a new topic, a new intellectual concept to consider. This would be wrong for our water cycle images, because each slide builds on the previous. A more appropriate transition might be Wipe, which smoothly wipes the new slide across the preceding one. The effect is of the first slide becoming the second — the new element appearing over the original picture. Since the basics of the images (mountains and ocean) are the same, the only thing that would change is the addition of a new image element — clouds. The first slide transitions should wipe left, since that is the direction of the cycle. The later slides should wipe right since the cycle has looped around to return to the ocean.

Every decision that we make about what we communicate and how we communicate it should be based on what we want to convey and what effect it should have on the audience. As I have already said in this chapter, this implies a different kind of assignment that gives the student a topic, an instructional goal, and an authentic audience, as well as information on how you want to affect that audience.

Communicating Compellingly —
Video Production

Of the information that we used during the last century, the medium that was most revered for its technique and technology was video. Most of us remember and probably still identify video production with huge cameras on rolling tripods or extensible conveyor arms, operated by highly trained professionals wired directly into a command booth. You might also imagine a small glassed-in room with an expansive array of controls, and video monitors with which technicians work wizardry on the images that we enjoyed.

This all changed in 1999 when Apple Computer introduced iMovie, a dramatically scaled-down video-editing program that was designed for ease of use rather than extensive visual effects. I already owned a digital video camera and had experimented with a desktop video-editing program for a number of years. I found video editing to be hard work, with a steep learning curve, and a wholly unsatisfying experience—not worth the time.

In 2001, I began shopping around for a new computer and was considering switching back to Macintosh. At that time, Apple was featuring iMovie in all of its advertisements, and even though the ads were quite impressive, my reaction was, "Is video editing a reason to buy a computer?" I finally decided to purchase a Macintosh, but not because of iMovie. It was Apple's new UNIX-based operating system that convinced me.

One afternoon, several weeks later, I had some time to play. Deciding to try out iMovie, I connected my digital video camera to my Mac notebook computer and proceeded to successfully capture and edit together about five minutes of video clips in less than 15 minutes—without needing any instructions. By the end of that afternoon, I decided that "Video editing is a very good reason to buy a computer." Before I turn this into an Apple commercial, it is important to note that many people have drawn this same conclusion, and there are now a number of easy-to-learn, easy-to-operate video-editing programs for Windows (I like Pinnacle Studio 8 for PCs) and Mac OS.

My conclusion about personal computers and video production is significant, and it has the potential to be the most crucial technology achievement in communication since the word processor. Telling a story or presenting a position by capturing and manipulating real-world imagery and motion with a $500 camera and editing software that comes pre-installed on many computers has the potential to change communication in ways that we cannot yet imagine. We know and accept that video is a powerful communicator. It teaches us by showing how the real world behaves not only across distance, but also across time. It is a means of multidimensional communication, and this is compelling.

Video is a form of communication that has laid a cultural backbone for generations of viewers, starting with my own. When my mother became pregnant with me, her first child, my parents bought their first TV, a Zenith 15 inch that they bought on an installment plan. They could watch only one channel that frequently displayed a test pattern. The only educational programming that was available to me was Captain Kangaroo, and I can still remember the sound of Bob Keeshan cutting construction paper with his scissors. Through this device, I grew up seeing people, places, and events that I will never visit in real life. I saw my own planet from outer space, men walking on the moon, dramatic portrayals of historic events, a nation in turmoil over a war, and the sanctioned mistreatment of our own citizens. My family received a view of our world that had never been available before and it affected us profoundly, and not always positively.

When my wife became pregnant with our first child, we bought our first VCR. This new technology gave us control over video viewing that my parents would not have imagined in the early '50s. What we viewed became our choice. For my children, it will be a tool for accomplishing goals.

Teaching students to use video will require some shifts in how we, as children of the twentieth century, view the technology. Once again, our tendency is to integrate video cameras and editing software into the school by producing a daily school news program from inside of a fashioned studio with news anchors, a director, camera people, and console technicians. This is not a bad way to use the technology, especially if all students are cycled through to benefit from all aspects of the production and as long as instructional objectives are a part of the process.

The problem with this application is that it is highly formatted. Each program will have the same or similar opening, broadcast sections (announcements, sports, in the news, weather, and so on), closing, and technical considerations for tying the production together. Because video production has become so cheap and easy to do, the ways that we use it will change, and we need to expand our image of video to become more of a personal means of communication (multicast) rather than thinking of it only in terms of the institutional publishing (broadcast).

Think about how you are currently asking students to demonstrate what they have learned, believe, and know, and imagine how they might express those ideas using video. A good way to do this is to watch documentaries on the Learning Channel, PBS, the History Channel, or other educational networks. The programs are essentially video research papers that overlay video on top of the words. Watch a documentary one evening and, as you are watching it, write down the ways that it is similar to the writing assignments you give your students and the ways that it is different. Think about asking your students to produce a video essay, or at least to think about how they would communicate the content in their written reports if they had access to video recording and editing technology.

Tom Sargent is a trainer for the Digital Storytelling project. He has worked with teachers and students on video production projects across the country through staff development that the organization offers for teachers and students. When shooting video, Mr. Sargent recommends that teachers stress planning, and that students should not be allowed to use photographic, video, or editing equipment until they have presented and defended their plans. At the same time, it is often necessary to assist student teams in keeping their planning to a simple and manageable level. He suggests that students be encouraged to use mind-mapping software during their planning process and that students be required to describe how each element of their plan addresses the target audience and goal.

After students have completed a proper plan, teachers should provide student teams with the equipment they need. When possible, arrange for students, who are supervised by the teacher, to do the training on the proper use of equipment and software. Students make good peer teachers when it comes to technology, and this reinforces understanding. One potential problem that often occurs can be overcome if the teacher requires a predetermined number of shots or video footage. This assures that the team has sufficient raw material to accomplish its goal.

For editing video, Mr. Sargent recommends using software that is easy to use and does not offer an overwhelming and distracting number of features. It is also essential that students are able to explain how each special effect or media addition enhances the message. He also suggests giving students a time limit so that they do not get bogged down in nuances.

Finally, Tom Sargent stresses that teachers should use video technology only when it enhances teaching and learning in identifiable ways. You can learn more about the Digital Storytelling project at its Web site: <http://www.digitalstorytelling.org>.

Once again, it all comes down to the assignment. If we merely ask students to report what they have learned, then they will learn little more than what is reportable. If we ask them to convince us of an idea, to affect our behavior in some way, then they will learn to use that knowledge. If we can give them the power to deliver a compelling message, then they become owners of that knowledge.

Communicating Compellingly — Web Publishing

Web pages are not a new format, but they are a new place, and this new place carries with it some unique characteristics and opportunities that must be understood in order to fully leverage this new communication medium. One of the unique qualities of Web publishing is its immediacy. When you create or edit the content or layout of your information, and upload the page to the Web server, both the publishing and distribution have instantly been achieved. It is immediately available to your information customers, as if it suddenly appeared on their desktops. Information publishing becomes more of a conversation because of this immediacy. However, getting your audience to listen/read and to return to the document for information updates is a different challenge. As mentioned earlier in this book, the technical aspects of publishing information on the Web are minor compared to the challenges of communicating.

Yet it is still important for educators to have some technical information that is essential for Web-based communication. Even though few people build Web pages with HTML (HyperText Markup Language), we will increasingly have opportunities to publish information on the Internet by merely typing our ideas into a Web form and clicking a submit button. Frequently called *content management systems*, many Web sites today are maintained in this way. The advantage of content management systems is speed and accessibility. Virtually anyone in your organization can publish his or her information to the Web site, any time, and from any Internet connected computer (see Figure 4.13 on page 78).

The downside is formatting. When entering Web content into a Web form, all that goes through are the words, and we have already explored how formatting (bold, italics, indention, and bullets) can cause information to communicate itself more effectively. To overcome this limitation, it is important for people to know a little bit of HTML, the language of the World Wide Web (see Figure 4.14 on page 79). If you can insert bolding, italics, or indention codes in with the ideas you type into the form, then you can increase the value of the information by making the information easier to read and understand.

You can practice your HTML coding using an interactive Web form on the page for this chapter at the Web site of this book: <http://landmark-project.com/redefining_literacy>.

Regardless of whether your students are creating a Web project or you are creating a classroom or school Web site, the most critical factor for producing a successful online document is planning. Planning can be done by an individual or team and it entails four steps:

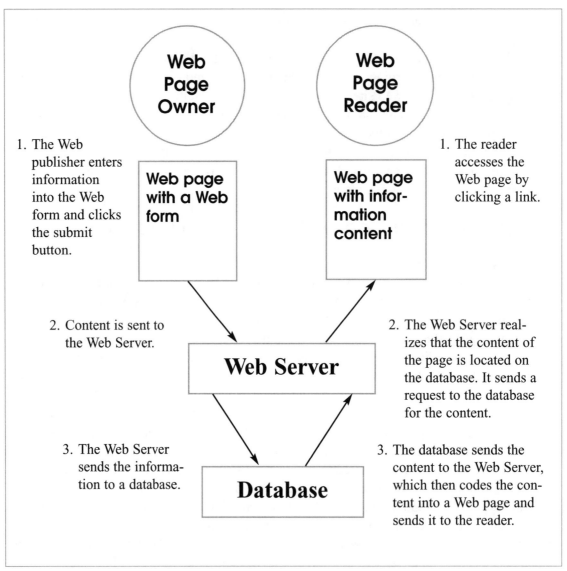

Figure 4.13: Content Management Systems

1. **Set Goals:** What do you want to accomplish with the Web site? What are your goals? It is critical that you plan for your goals by listing those things that your information customers can do to help you accomplish your goals. Write a list of those actions and behaviors that will help you do your job.
2. **Select Content:** What information should you publish to accomplish your goals? Think, again, of your information customers and their desired behaviors. You need to identify information that will provoke those behaviors and assist your customers in accomplishing them.
3. **Plan Strategy:** How should your information appear on the screen? Information design is probably the most difficult part of building a Web site. We have already listed some of the ways that text can be formatted to communicate itself more effectively. Also consider if information will communicate itself better as a picture, graph, chart, table, sound, or video. It is about communication.
4. **Act:** Implement your plan, evaluate for success, and adapt.

HTML All Teachers Should Know

Basics	▪ All HTML codes (called tags) are enclosed inside of angle brackets <tag>. ▪ Most tags include a beginning and ending tag. The beginning tag signals that formatting should begin here. The ending tags signals where the formatting should end. ▪ Beginning tags consist only of the tag inside of angle brackets <tag>. ▪ Ending tags are preceded by a forward slash (/) all inside of angle brackets </tag>. ▪ HTML tags can be either upper- or lowercase.
Bold Text	The bold tag is the letter "<B>". When the bold tag is placed in your text, the following letters will be bolded in the Web page. Bolding will end where the ending bold tag is placed. `Here is some <b>bold</b> text!`
Italics	The italics tag is the letter "<i>". When the italics tag is placed in your text, the following letters will be italicized in the Web page. Italics will end where the ending italics tag is placed. `Here is some <i>italic</i> text!`
Line Breaks	There are two ways to produce a line break. Placing the break tag " " at the end of an intended line will force the following text to the next line. Placing a paragraph tag "<p>" at the end of an intended paragraph will force the following text to the next line skipping a line, creating some white space between the paragraphs.
Indent	There are two ways to indent text. The Blockquote tag will indent text at both the left and right margins. Simply place the "<blockquote>" tag at the beginning of a paragraph and the ending "</blockquote>" tag at the end of the paragraph. The second way to indent text is to use the directory tag. This will indent text at only the left margin. Simply place the "<dir>" tag at the beginning of a paragraph and the ending "</dir>" tag at the end of the paragraph.

Bulleted List	The bulleted list is slightly more complicated. First you have to mark the list with the "<ul>" or Unordered List tag. Place the beginning tag "<ul>" at the top of the list and the ending tag "</ul>" at the bottom of the list.
	    Then mark each list item with the "<li>" or List Item tag. Place the beginning "<li>" tag at the beginning of each item and the ending tag "</li>" at the end of each item.
	`Here are my favorite colors`
	`<ul>`
	`<li>Blue,</li>`
	`<li>Red,</li>`
	`<li>Yellow, and</li>`
	`<li>Green</li>`
	`</ul>`

Hyperlink	The heart of the World Wide Web is our ability to connect documents together. To create a hyperlink within your text, place the anchor or "<a>" tag in front of the clickable text and the ending anchor or "</a>" tag at the end. Then you must add some additional information to the beginning tag, an attribute. After the beginning tag, add a space and href= and the URL of the page you wish to link to. `The Web site at <a href=http://www.loc.gov>Library of Congress</a> has information that may be useful to you.`

Figure 4.14: HTML for Teachers

I want to add one note about creating a classroom or school Web site. If you do not have one, make one, and use the planning process above to accomplish it. Building a Web page is not difficult, especially if your district can employ a content management system to support teacher Web publishing.

Your classroom Web site is a window on your classroom. It reveals what and how you are teaching, and how well your students are learning. Frankly, Web publishing can more effectively serve as an accountability method than annual standardized tests. Your students' parents and your community want pictures, ideas, and stories, and they want to see results more than they want to see statistics.

Finally, a classroom or school Web site will help you do your job—if you plan. If you want to see students take greater care with their homework assignments, post assignment details and policies on your site. If you want to involve parents in special projects, but limit how they are to contribute, publish the project details and specify how parents and other caregivers can support the students in their work. If you want to improve the efficiency of getting students off the campus and on their way home after school, then publish a map of the parking and pickup areas with clear instructions on how parents should pick up their children; format the page so that it can be printed and carried in the door pocket of a car. Web publishing solves problems and accomplishes goals—when we plan with these ends in mind.

Communicating Compellingly — Programming

In conclusion, I would like to add one more type of communication—talking to your computer in its language. Am I suggesting that we should all become programmers? Of course not. Most of us do not have the temperament to sit and write computer code all day, but there are two important reasons why we and our students should have some experience in programming computers.

First of all, learning to program a computer helps to demystify the tool. Computers can appear to be almost magical to us. However, their wizardry comes from highly complex arrangements of very simple instructions: add, subtract, remember, and display. If students have some experience in commanding their computers at this basic level, they will see the machine for what it is, a tool.

The second reason that students should have some experience with programming is that some of them will be programmers in the future. Part of the power of the computer is the fact that we can transform it into many different things by the instructions we give it, and if we can instruct the machine, we can shape it into tools that help us on a personal level. One very general example of this is the spreadsheet. Many of us use spreadsheets, but few of us have created our own spreadsheet files to solve unique problems in very customized ways. A major airline recently lost my luggage during a multi-leg flight to New York (the first loss of luggage in eight years of frequent traveling). Fortunately, I had insurance with my credit card company that allowed me to quickly replace items that were immediately essential. Since I was flying to Chicago the next day, I had to replace the luggage, toiletries, razor, suit, and so on. Unfortunately, my insurance only covered $300 worth of emergency purchases. I created a spreadsheet that enabled me to enter the items I needed and their prices and then check the items by priority in order to stay below $300 and still make my trip in some sense of comfort. As it turned out, I wore a sport coat instead of a new suit in Chicago, as well as an old belt. My bags turned up more than a week later after bouncing back and forth between Atlanta and Newark. I asked for frequent flyer miles, but to no avail. The point is that I was able to shape the computer into a tool that helped me solve a specific problem.

Apple Computer introduced HyperCard in 1987. Designed to allow anyone to create small applications to perform specific tasks, HyperCard gave thousands of people the ability to shape their computers for their needs. Much could be done simply by pulling down menus, adding buttons, and describing what should happen as a result of clicking those buttons. However, there was a simple, yet powerful programming language associated with HyperCard, called *HyperTalk*. With HyperTalk, a Mac user could create small but sophisticated personal applications. Since the early Internet was almost exclusively associated with UNIX and Macintosh computers, the earliest HTML editors were personal HyperCard tools created by their users.

It may be something of a stretch, but part of enjoying our technology will be in customizing it to address our personal needs and interests. It is about finding the truth in information, employing that truth, and communicating our conclusions.

Conclusion

Earlier in this book, mention was made of a recent world record in data transmitted over the Internet. Scientists at Stanford University successfully sent 6.7 gigabytes of data from California to the Netherlands in less than one minute. To put this into perspective, 6.7 gigabytes is the equivalent of 200 sets of encyclopedias. Now just imagine what you could do with 200 sets of encyclopedias coming into your computers in less than one minute. If you cannot think of that much, then my point is made. Who can handle that much text — that fast? However, when we equate 6.7 gigabytes to roughly four hours of DVD quality video in less than a minute, possibilities begin to emerge: motion pictures, multimedia manuals, virtual field trips, rich education, all on demand. The point is that we are not producing this amazing capacity to communicate in order to send e-mails or other forms of text. We are producing this capacity for multimedia, because we know that it is with multimedia that people will be communicating in the twenty-first century.

It will be our students who are filling this capacity, so it is essential that at the same time that we teach them to write, we also teach them to communicate with images, animation, sound, and video.

Action Items

Directors of Technology

- Explore, plan, and implement venues for teachers to display student-produced information products. Collaborate with the local public library, community college, banks, and other places to display student productions.
- Offer staff development opportunities for teachers and students on computer graphics, Web design, information layout, music composition, and video production. Be careful that the focus is always communication rather than the technology.
- Assist school principals, tech facilitators, media specialists, and teachers in planning for integrating computer-assisted production in their instructional process.

- Work to provide appropriate hardware and software in sufficient quantities so that teachers can conveniently implement their plans.
- Establish a district Web site that is designed to showcase student (and teacher) products on an ongoing basis. Provide opportunities for the public to comment on the work (via Web forms) and post appropriate comments along with the productions.
- Work toward placing graphic software on every computer, digital still and video cameras in every classroom, and numerous music composition stations in every school.

Principals

- Understand that the accountability that parents and the community truly want to see is what their teachers are teaching, how they are teaching it, what students are learning, and how they are learning it. Look for opportunities to showcase exemplary examples of each to your community and leverage those opportunities.
- Plan a school Web site and a way for all teachers and other professional staff members to publish information to that site. Require that all teachers have classroom Web sites and demonstrate how their Web sites help them do their job.
- Think of your school as more than its building. Include in your vision of the school all of the information products (text, images, songs, video) that are produced by students and teachers. Help the community to include these products in its vision of the school.
- Work with the media specialist, tech facilitator, teachers, and central office staff to plan for wise and sufficient procurement of hardware and software. Integrate information production into the teaching and learning process.
- Invite community comments on student and teacher work.
- Establish a video production team and school photographers and assign them with the responsibility to record the significant events of the school year. Have both upperclassmen and underclassmen on the team so that experienced students train less experienced students. Assign supervision to the media specialist and tech facilitator.

Media Specialists

- Assist the principal in planning and implementing the school's Web site.
- Include in your media center Web site a section that showcases student productions.
- Establish displays in the media center (and beyond) for showcasing student productions.
- Establish an archive of student productions, both digital and non-digital, and catalog them so that students and teachers have access to their work. Include with each product all of its authors and their specific contributions. Make these products available to future students for improvement.
- Work with the tech facilitator (or music teacher) to establish a music production station in the media center. As student teams produce musical selections, archive and catalog them with other students' productions.

- Work with the tech facilitator to form media production clubs in your school for still photography, video production, music production, animation, and so on.

School Tech Facilitators

- Assist the principal and media specialist in planning and implementing the school's Web site.
- Establish a music production station in the media center; train selected students to use the hardware and software and help them to form a team to serve as consultants to other students in producing music for their presentations and other information products. (If the school has a music teacher, this function should be performed by that person.)
- Assist the principal and media specialist in procurement of production hardware and software by compiling an ongoing folder of specifications and reviews (formal and casual) of various media production equipment and software.
- Establish an inventory of hardware and software and implement a checkout plan that makes it easy for teachers to acquire additional equipment when needed. Make sure that each teacher has access to cameras in his or her classroom at all times, software for downloading images from the cameras, and training to operate the cameras and software.
- Establish a mailing list for teachers for sharing information about production tools, techniques, and experiences of students creating information products for class work.
- Work with the media specialist to form media production clubs in your school for still photography, video production, music production, animation, and so on.

Teachers

- In your classroom, have a charged digital video camera at your disposal at all times. Be ready at any time to take pictures of events that might be useful in the future. Think of it as a note-taking tool.
- When going on a field trip, have numerous digital still and video cameras available to students for recording important aspects of the trip.
- Allow students to select information products that were constructed by past students and improve on their work as a way of completing assignments.
- Coordinate with the media specialists on the creation of a library of student productions.
- Identify students with a particular interest in music, and connect them with a media specialist or tech facilitator for training on music compositions.

Students

- As you watch movies, TV programs, documentaries, or listen to music, ask yourself these questions:
  - In what ways did this performance affect what I know and believe?
  - How did the performance accomplish this effect?

- In what ways did this performance affect me emotionally?
- How did the performance accomplish this effect?
- What visual or auditory effects did the director or producer employ that were especially effective?

■ Join clubs related to media production (video, photography, graphic, text, music).

■ As you are learning to use production hardware and software, imagine how the equipment or software might be improved in the future to make the process easier or more powerful.

■ When you know that programs will be occurring on TV or in the movie theatre that are related in some way to your classroom studies, tell your teachers and ask if you can get extra credit for viewing them and then reporting on what you learned.

■ If you are especially interested in video production, art, music composition, or photography, work toward acquiring your own equipment and software, and develop your skills. Have fun doing it.

Parents

■ Visit your school's Web site regularly and view its showcase of student productions. If there is an opportunity, make productive comments about the works.

■ If you have some knowledge, skill, or experience in media production of any type, volunteer your time at the school to help students and teachers learn from your expertise.

■ If your children express a special interest in video production, art, music composition, or photography, help them acquire their own equipment and software, and develop your skills as well.

■ If you do not have one already, purchase a digital still or video camera and begin a library of family events.

5 Ethics and Context

W e find ourselves working and playing within an information environment. It has natural laws and tendencies. It operates well under some conditions, and not so well under others. Also, in the same way that the natural environment can be threatened by counter ecological actions, our information environment is equally fragile. We have existed and prospered within an information environment for many years and our definitions of literacy have described those skills and knowledge that are necessary in order to succeed within this environment. Before information imposed itself as a dominant feature of our environment, literacy described the degree to which we could use the land and the seasons to raise food and cash crops. Today, our success depends on how well we can use the information around us and profit from its continuous change.

Ethics and the Age of Information

Literacy describes skills and knowledge. It also describes behaviors related to how we leverage our environment in order to exist and prosper. Historically, as people and communities became socially and economically interconnected and dependent on each other, margins of behavior were set. They defined acts that were detrimental to people and their communities. For instance, if one farmer stole crops from another or ranchers dammed up a river that irrigated farmland, it had direct and negative impacts on people, families, and communities who depended on the land for their existence and prosperity. Also, if an agricultural community planted the same crops year after year without attention to replenishing the nutrients in the soil, it had an ultimately devastating impact on the well-being of all of its members.

Making appropriate use of natural resources could be characterized as a corridor through which responsible behaviors were practiced for the good of all. On either side of that corridor were margins of irresponsible behavior that harmed other people or wasted natural resources and opportunities. Likewise, there is a corridor of responsible behaviors with regard to information, along with margins of inappropriate and dangerous behaviors. Drawing the line between these actions continues to be a challenge.

Consider the story of Christine Pelton, a former biology teacher in Piper, Kansas. It is a story you have probably already heard, but it bears repeating within the context of defining our corridor of acceptable behavior. Ms. Pelton had a rule in her classroom. If students plagiarized, they received a zero for the work. This was a hard rule, and students and parents signed contracts acknowledging this rule. The last assignment that Ms. Pelton made was called the "Leaf Project." Students were required to collect leaves from 20 local trees and report on each. When the reports were turned in, she found that many of the written reports had identical sentences and some of the writing was not consistent with the normal writing levels of her students. She took the reports to **TurnItIn.com** <http://www.turnitin.com>, an online plagiarism detection service, and found evidence that 28 of the students had plagiarized information from the Internet in their reports. These students received failing grades for their work.

The principal of the school supported Christine in her grading. However, under pressure from the students' parents and the suggestion of the superintendent, the school board ruled that the students should receive a failing grade only for the research part of the assignment (about 40%) and that the weighting of the project be reduced so that the students would pass for the semester. The day after the ruling, Christine Pelton resigned. Before the beginning of the next school year, Christine's principal also resigned along with 30% of the district's other teachers and counselors because the story, which went national, devastated the community's reputation. The superintendent eventually resigned under a settlement agreement.

What played out in Piper, Kansas, was an inevitable clash between an older twentieth century attitude toward information and a newer twenty-first century information environment. The pivotal point is that sometime between the schooling of their parents and the educational environment promoted by Christine Pelton, the value of information changed. During the 1950s and '60s, when I was in school, the information economy was based on a medieval structure. The producers and distributors of information were a restrictive nobility of powerful publishers and networks who produced and distributed information to the rest of us, the vast information consumers. This relationship between a few information producers and a multitude of consumers was out of balance, from our perspective, especially as information was already beginning to play a crucial part in our lives. As information users, we felt victimized by price-fixing, editorializing, commercial interests, and a catering to the lowest common denominator of consumer interests.

This imbalance of power between information producers and consumers gave us, the victims, the right to do with information what we wanted. We were taught not to copy text from the encyclopedia; but if we exercised the semantics of paraphrasing, then it was OK to use the information of others. We were taught how to create a bibliography, but not why. I graduated from high school believing that the only place you cited information resources was in research papers. I was also fairly sure that I would be writing my last research paper sometime in the next four years, so citing resources was seen as an exclusively academic exercise.

Information is changing, not only in where you find it and what it looks like, but also where it comes from. We will all be information producers and, thanks to the Internet, information distributors. My own Web site receives over six million page views a month from nearly 100 countries. This is information that is produced and distributed by one person from a basement office. The fact that each of us can publish information and distribute it to a global audience dramatically changes the balance between producer and consumer. When the information that we consider using may have been produced at great effort by another teacher, student, neighbor, or family member, we will consider the ownership of that information in a different way. Few of us would cheat a neighbor in the same way we may be willing to cheat a large multinational corporation.

Christine Pelton understood this and insisted that her students respect information as valuable property that was owned by somebody else. The parents who appealed to the board of education to change Ms. Pelton's grading policy treated information as an abundant commodity whose ownership and credit is less important than its availability. Neither is at fault. It is a sign of the rapidly changing nature of information.

The best way to help students understand and appreciate information as valuable property is to make them property owners. Under the new copyright law, the **Digital Millennium Copyright Act of 1998**, all information is assumed to be copyrighted unless specifically labeled otherwise. All formal documents, informal notes, e-mails, and student works are automatically copyrighted. To use information created by someone else requires permission that is either granted as a courtesy or purchased. Documents are not required to display the ubiquitous copyright message in order to be considered copyrighted, although the message may still be included.

Placing this designation does convey a sense of property and importance to a document and respect for its author. When students complete an information product, whether it be a poem, report, Web page, multimedia presentation, or story, ask them to label their ownership of the document by placing the copyright text at the bottom of their pages: *Copyright © 2003 by John Doe.*

We should also develop the habit of talking about students' works as belonging to them. Rather than referring to "this paper," we should say, "your paper." When evaluating their multimedia presentation, we should talk about it being their message, their report, or their document. We should also overtly ask for students' permission before using any parts of their work as examples either in class or as part of a student showcase.

Another quality of information products is infinite expandability. In the working world, information products are rarely created in a vacuum. We are always building on the work of others. We start with this report, adapt that curriculum, update a five-year-old policy, or combine the writings of several experts into a well-crafted, persuasive message. Expecting students to always start an information project from the beginning is not an authentic simulation of the workplace. It would be more realistic to give them an existing document with instructions to expand this information product to add these features or present this perspective.

This can be easily accomplished by establishing a library of student-produced information products that have been completed and evaluated, and then archived for future use. The work that students perform has value to future students and teachers, and the authors will continue to receive credit for their contributions. For instance, if a middle-school class is studying volcanoes, the teacher might hand to a student a printed report that was written and turned in the previous year along with a digital version of the report. As an assignment, the teacher might ask the student to use the content from the report and produce a multimedia presentation that enhances the ideas through images, animation, sound, and video. It becomes an activity of research, organization, and media production. Another student might be given a multimedia presentation and asked to write and attach text that complements the existing media, providing conceptual explanations for the presentation. In each scenario, the student is building on the work of previous students, producing a far more important and powerful work as a result. All students, past and present, would receive credit appropriate to their contributions. An important function of librarians would be to curate libraries of student work that can be used as assignment starters or as instructional products by teachers.

Plagiarism is bad. Using the information of other people within the confines of copyright law is not. Building on the work of others adds value. Crediting the work of others makes them your partners. When reading, evaluating, and studying various information products as a matter of course, we should help students to discover the value that they have for other people. We produce information to help people make decisions, to establish a personal sense of who, where, and when they are, or to entertain. If it accomplishes these goals, then it has value.

The value of information also comes from its authority. If the content comes from a recognized or credentialed authority on the topic, then its reliability and value are increased. As we evaluate our students' works, a large part of the evaluation should be based on the value or potential value of the products.

- Who is its intended audience?
- In what ways might it benefit them?
- How successful was the student or team of students in accomplishing the goal?
- To what degree has the product been enhanced with authority?

If students understand that employing the assistance of experts in their information products adds to the value of their work, and consequently a more favorable evaluation, then they may be more likely to properly cite the work of others. We should shift away from paraphrasing as a way of permitting the use of other people's intellectual property and toward citation.

This does not mean that students should stop paraphrasing or otherwise use their own writing. As one who taught in the twentieth century, I know that we had students paraphrase information in order to assure that they read and understood the content they were using. Shifting to citation also does not mean that students should copy and paste huge chunks of copyrighted information and turn it in. We want students to work with information in ways that accomplish instructional goals. We also want students to work toward goals that they can identify with, goals that make sense to their current and perceived future experiences. The answer is to give a different kind of assignment. Asking students to merely write a report about a topic makes sense from a purely instructional viewpoint but little sense to students who are learning how to interact with the world around them. Basic reports on teacher assigned topics also make it too easy for students to copy large chunks of text or images and paste them into their word processors. Even if the student does cite the resources, he or she may not have truly examined the information nor learned how it impacts his or her life.

If the student is assigned to produce an information product for a specific audience and with a specific goal in mind, and the teacher's evaluation of the product will at least partly be based on the intrinsic value of the work, then the student will need to:

- Find information that supports his or her task,
- Decode and evaluate the information,
- Assemble it in a way that addresses the audience and goal, and
- Publish the information in a medium that will most likely result in success.

Sometimes the information the student collects will best serve the purpose of the assignment unaltered. Often the student will paraphrase the information in a way that is more consistent with his or her audience and goal. Remember the building blocks of information that students mine and assemble, and the mortar that they must mix and lay. Students are still working with the information. They are simply doing so within a more authentic context. You can read about a few sample authentic assignments in figure 5.1.

The assignments are not new, nor are they especially creative. However, they all involve an authentic audience and a meaningful goal for that audience. The authenticity of

Some Authentic Assignments Based on Curriculum Standards

Grade Level & Subject	Standard	Assignment
Grade 3 Healthful Living	The learner will direct personal health behaviors in accordance with his or her own health status and susceptibility to major health risks.	Ask students to develop a poster with a set of rules for personal behavior for a local summer camp to be printed and displayed in camp cabins. Audience: Young campers Goal: Prevent potential health problems
Grade 4 Mathematics	Spatial Sense, Measurement, and Geometry — The learner will demonstrate an understanding and use of the properties and relationships in geometry, as well as the standard units of metric and customary measurement.	Ask teams of students to create a blueprint for the school of the future. Ask them to base their design on interviews with students and teachers. Audience: School planners of the future Goal: Promote schools that are student and teacher centered
Grade 5 Music	The learner will compose and arrange music within specified guidelines.	Ask students to compose and record an original musical piece to accompany a multimedia presentation they are creating for another subject. Audience: Other students Goal: Depends on the multimedia assignment
Grade 6 Science	Describe ways in which organisms interact with each other and with non-living parts of the environment: ▪ Limiting factors ▪ Coexistence/Cooperation/ Competition ▪ Symbiosis	Select a geographic area that is currently undeveloped. Ask students to research the impact of urban development on the ecosystem, and then project the potential impact of development in the selected area. Audience: Urban planners and voters Goal: Promote development that is less detrimental to the environment
Grade 7 Social Studies	Geography — The learner will locate major physical features and suggest the influence of their location on life in Africa and Asia.	Research the physical features of a country in Africa or Asia and then design and produce a brochure for a tourist company. Audience: Vacationers Goal: Persuade vacationers to visit the assigned country
Grade 9–12 Second Languages	The learner will engage in conversation and exchange information and opinions orally and in writing in the target language.	Establish a relationship with a class in a country that speaks the target language. Agree upon an issue and then require students to send messages in the target language that explain their country's position on the issue. Audience: Students in another country with a different language Goal: Share national perspectives

Figure 5.1: Authentic Assignments

the assignment forces students to do a very important thing. They must think about the information they are considering and make decisions on where, how, and why it will be used. This is a powerful learning action.

Understanding information as valuable property is only one part of addressing an information revolution that has occurred within just one generation—and its ethical implications. Consider that in 2002, a handful of corporate executives, in an attempt to deceive stockholders and employees, succeeded in bringing the U.S. economy to its knees. Certainly the dot.com meltdown, attack of September 11, and subsequent war in Iraq contributed to the persistently weak economy of 2002 and 2003. However, the deceptive actions of these few very powerful people pulled the foundation out from under the economy—a foundation of trust.

When information becomes the glue that holds together our business and social institutions, that information must be rock-solid reliable, and this reliability is no less important than that of our traditional infrastructure: our roads, bridges, buildings, and power lines. Our information infrastructure was seriously eroded by the 2002 scandals caused by greed and a disregard for the truth. Over the past two decades, success has been defined in terms of the windfalls, IPOs, corporate culture, and early retirement. These were the measure of success, and succeeding in these terms outweighed the integrity that clearly characterized previous generations. As one Piper High School student said, "... I would say that in this day and age, cheating is almost not wrong. Because it is any way that you can get an advantage." These are words spoken by a student of the '80s and '90s. At the same time that we teach students the value of information, it is absolutely necessary that we teach the value of the truth. Information is the foundation of our institutions today, and that foundation is only as sturdy as it is truthful.

Information is also powerful, and twenty-first century literacy equips students and adults with powerful tools. We have at our disposal a global electronic library of raw information. We are increasingly gaining access to powerful computers that can alter that information in infinite ways. We are also learning to communicate our ideas in highly compelling formats that influence and even manipulate other people. Consider that in the 1920s and 1930s, a relatively unassuming young man changed a nation from one that was reeling from a devastating military defeat and subsequent humiliation to one that was nearly able to conquer a continent, while at the same time implementing an unprecedented, factory-like extermination of millions of people. Adolf Hitler accomplished this by using information to influence people's beliefs and feelings. To implement a new and potent literacy without considering this darker side could be tragic.

To make some sense of information ethics, I want to return to one of the shifts in the nature of information that was described earlier in this book. In the last 10 years we have seen an enormous shift from a purely broadcast society (production and distribution of information by a few) to a multicast society (production and distribution of information by many/all). To explore the ethical responsibilities of information workers, I want to step back to the broadcast model and examine one of the primary sources of content at this time— journalists. It is the job of journalists to collect information about conditions in our social, cultural, and physical environments and report on them in a way that their readers continue to be informed as democratic citizens. Their job is to *expose the truth*, *employ information*, and *express ideas compellingly*.

Journalists aspire to high standards of ethics, reflecting the importance of their mission and the potential harm that is possible from irresponsible practices. To define these standards, the Society of Professional Journalists (SPJ) has published a code of ethics for its members. You can read this code at its Web site: <http://www.spj.org/ethics_code.asp>.

Perhaps more than any other profession, journalism has practiced, for many years, the level of literacy that is relevant for all of us in the twenty-first century. Journalists seek out information, decode it, evaluate, process, and communicate it in compelling ways. For this reason, I am using the SPJ's code of ethics as a springboard to model an information code of ethics for teachers and students. It addresses the issues of truth and also the potential power of information to do both good and harm. The major goals of this code of ethics are:

1. To describe a desire to seek and share the truth of any issue, understanding that the truth extends far beyond the mere accuracy of facts.
2. To minimize the harm that may result from the expression of information.
3. To apply accountability to information producers and users for the outcomes of their work.
4. To guard the information infrastructure from physical or digital breakdown.

Goal number one describes a need to pursue the truth. Are we going to answer the question, "What is truth?" No! Such questions are left up to philosophers. However, it is necessary that we expand our notions of truth and the specific issues that cradle it. Truth, in a time of nearly ubiquitous access to global information and our increasing ability to produce and distribute compelling content, is more than factual accuracy. The accuracy of a piece of information only points to its nature as an isolated piece of data. This limited version of truth can be used quite effectively to influence people's beliefs and even their decisions. It happens every day through advertising, both commercial and political. The total meaning of accurate information includes the nature of its real and potential impact on people. The reckless and irresponsible use of accurate facts can cause great harm.

When considering the truth of information, students and teachers must be able to answer these questions in addition to whether it is accurate:

1. Under what conditions will the information remain accurate? Will it be accurate tomorrow? Is it accurate from relevant perspectives (Middle Eastern, African, consumer, employee, young, old, and so on)?
2. Will communicating the information in the way that you are considering cause harm or threaten harm to any one person or group of people?
3. Will not communicating the information in the way that you are considering cause harm or threaten harm to any one person or group of people?
4. How will communicating the information positively impact any one person or group of people?

The second goal speaks directly to the intended or inadvertent consequences of information. Compellingly expressed information has the power to affect how people feel, what they believe, the decisions they make, and how they interact with other people. There is enormous potential for improving our condition with information, and equal potential for harm and suffering. This potential must be a part of every decision made with regard to information. Another aspect of this goal is respect for other people's intellectual property. Compiling information, processing it, and building a new and valuable information product is hard work. This makes information valuable, at least to the builder, and absolutely essential that credit be given to the owners of all information that is used.

The third goal of an information code of ethics refers to accountability. The journalist holds herself or himself accountable by applying a byline to his or her report. Journalists are putting their reputations behind their information products and making themselves available to defend their work. In order to assure the safe use of information, those who access, employ, and express it must be accountable for their actions and the outcomes. This means that any information work must include, as an essential component, the author's willingness to defend the work in terms of its truthfulness and the harm it might cause. All information products should include supporting information, or references to supporting information about the content, so that consumers can evaluate the quality of the product for themselves.

The final element of an information code of ethics deals with the information infrastructure on which our civilization has come to depend so heavily. This information foundation is only as dependable as the hardware and software of the computers and networks where they reside and interact, and these facilities are vulnerable. During the final edit of this book, we were all reeling from the effects of the SoBig virus that impacted not only those computers that were infected, but also many more people as the code was written to attribute the spread of the virus to e-mail addresses taken randomly from address books. Even though I use a Macintosh, which is immune to most viruses, my mailbox was flooded with e-mails automatically issued by mail-managing software alerting me that I had sent a virus. During this time, I was working in northern Wisconsin where I did not have access to e-mail. My mailbox filled up with SoBig related e-mail, causing messages from clients, colleagues, and associates to bounce back as if I no longer existed. This, of course, could affect my income as an independent consultant. We must set standards of behavior that protect this infrastructure and creatively eliminate the desire in people to cause mayhem in cyberspace.

Following is a code of ethics that has been adapted from the one published by the Society of Professional Journalists. This is intended as a model or starting point for information guidelines for your teachers and students:

A Student & Teacher's Information Code of Ethics

Seek Truth and Express It

Teachers and students should be honest, fair, and courageous in gathering, interpreting, and expressing information for the benefit of others. They should:

- Test the accuracy of information from all sources and exercise care to avoid inadvertent error.
- Always identify sources. The consumers of your information product must be able to make their own judgment of its value.
- Always question the sources' motives.
- Never distort or misrepresent the content of photos, videos, or other media without an explanation of intent and permission from the information's owner. Image enhancement for technical clarity is permissible.
- Tell the story of the human experience boldly, even when it is unpopular to do so.
- Examine your own cultural values and avoid imposing those values on others.

- Avoid stereotyping by race, gender, age, religion, ethnicity, geography, sexual orientation, disability, physical appearance, or social status.
- Give voice to the voiceless; official and unofficial sources of information can be equally valid.
- Distinguish between opinion and fact when expressing ideas. Analysis and commentary should be labeled and not misrepresent fact or context.

Minimize Harm

Ethical teachers and students treat information sources, subjects, colleagues, and information consumers as human beings deserving of respect.

- Gathering and expressing information should never cause harm or threaten to be harmful to any one person or group of people.
- Recognize that private people in their private pursuits have a greater right to control information about themselves than do others.
- Consider all possible outcomes to the information you express, guarding against potential harm to others.
- Never use information from another person without proper citation and permission.

Be Accountable

Teachers and students are accountable to their readers, listeners, and viewers and to each other.

- Clarify and explain information and invite dialogue about your conduct as a communicator.
- Encourage the information consumer to voice grievances about your information products.
- Admit mistakes and correct them promptly.
- Expose unethical information practices of others.

Respect Information and its Infrastructure

Information, in the Information Age, is property. Information is the fabric that defines much of what we do from day to day, and this rich and potent fabric is fragile.

- Never undertake any action that has the potential to damage any part of this information infrastructure. These actions include, but are not limited to, illegally hacking into a computer system, launching or distributing viruses or other damaging software, physically damaging or altering hardware or software, or publishing information that you know is untrue or potentially harmful.
- Report to proper authorities any activities that could potentially result in harm to the information infrastructure.

There are two terms that are used numerous times in the code of ethics above, and both have been used in other places in the book. Both terms have been used in other publications and discussions, but they do bear further explanation within the context of this book.

They are *information product* and *information consumer.* Both terms owe their phrasing to the notion that information will be the raw material with which most people will work during the Information Age, and with this information raw material, we will construct a wide variety of information products which people will consume—information consumers.

During the twentieth century, we could talk about students' writings, or art, or projects. However, today we may refer to a much wider and richer array of products when describing their work. It may be writing or art. However, the work may manifest itself as a Web page, or multimedia production using presentation software. It may be a virtual reality experience, a performance, or a piece of software. Each of these is a product that, when constructed with an audience and a goal in mind, can be used or consumed by people.

Teaching students how to produce information may lead to them becoming more responsible consumers of information.

Context

It is this section of the book that may stray farthest from twentieth century notions of education, and yet the terms of this discussion will likely be most familiar to educators and non-educators alike. Thus far, we have explored a new definition of literacy that expands out of the three "Rs" of the previous century. It is important to reemphasize that this new vision of literacy, the ability to *expose information, employ information, express ideas compellingly,* and finally integrate an ethical code into our use of information, constitutes not only a set of "basic skills" for the twenty-first century, but also a **Learning Literacy** that is essential to personal growth in a future where learning is a way of life. There is a great deal said at education conferences and planning meetings about online courses and distance learning, and their importance in a future of life-long learning. Remote teaching and learning is now and will continue to be a crucial part of the education landscape of the twenty-first century. However, the biggest part of distance learning will be much more casual. It will simply mean being able to find the information that you need in order to do what you need to do—right now. This involves exposing the information in a global electronic library, employing that information, and expressing what you have learned in compelling ways. If you can do this, you are literate (See figure 5.2).

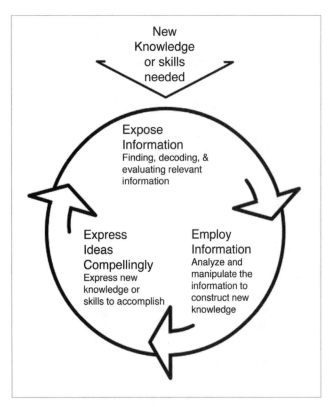

Figure 5.2: Learning Literacy

If it is true that we will learn throughout our lives in order to continue to be economically viable and to function appropriately and enjoyably in an increasingly information-driven and technology-rich world, what else should our children be learning while they are in our schools becoming literate? Education has operated under the belief that there is a definable and finite body of knowledge that students should learn, and that gaining this knowledge will lead to success in their adulthood. Today, we call them standards.

The core literacies of the twentieth century were reading, writing, and mathematics. These were the information skills that were necessary to be economically and politically competent during that time. However, we also taught science, history, health, music, and art. We did this in order to provide for our students a **context** for their lives, to give them a sense of who, where, and when they are.

This literacy of context will change the least of all of the others. Reading, math, and writing expand into new sets of skills that were simply irrelevant in the twentieth century. What we teach our students in order to build a context for their lives and their future will remain largely the same in form, though how we teach and assess it should change dramatically.

Even though the main areas of focus in providing a context for our students will probably not change, we must create learning experiences for our students that are sensitive to the actuality that the facts that we are teaching may not be true 10 years from now. Consider the challenges of teaching physics when discoveries in quantum mechanics are forcing us to redefine the nature of reality. Consider biology when work in genetics is changing our deepest beliefs about life and longevity. Consider the potential impact of nanotechnology on nearly all aspects of our lives—nanoassemblers that build for us one molecule at a time, or nanobots in our blood stream carrying away cholesterol and other harmful agents. Then consider all of the possibilities and opportunities in the near future that we cannot even imagine.

What about social studies and literature? If we look at the true, day-to-day challenges that face this world, they are not problems of science and mathematics, but of people getting along with other people. How do you teach geography, economics, and history in ways that equip our children to solve these problems? What literature prepares students for a rapidly changing world?

The classrooms of the twentieth century were intended to prepare students for a workplace characterized by working in straight rows, performing repetitive tasks under close supervision. Their design was based on a vision of orderly mechanization, sequenced processes, and the assembly of distinct though connected pieces—a vision that deeply characterized the times.

In the highly regimented classrooms of the twentieth century and the focus on quality control that emerged in the past decade, the context subjects have largely been reduced to a series of facts that are available for recall and bubbling. This is not to say that good teachers are no longer teaching higher-order appreciations and the intrinsic joy of learning. It does not mean that library media specialists are not creating valuable research and learning environments that support and challenge students to teach themselves. However, these realms of learning and teaching are severely threatened by the standards movement of the 1990s, as teachers struggle to squeeze more and more content into the year under increased accountability through standardized tests. As our changing world has added to what we believe our children should know, little is being removed. Culling out the portions of our curricula that are no longer essential is no small task, nor is it a new concern. Yet when we remind ourselves of how much childhood today is spent in pursuit of our curricula, it becomes more apparent that we need to relieve our children of many of the expectations we are requiring of them in the name of *high standards*.

Large Idea!

The classrooms of the 20th century were intended to prepare students for a workplace characterized by working in straight rows, performing repetitive tasks under close supervision.

Consider those skills and knowledge that you were required to prove that you had learned in school and then ask yourself how much of it you simply do not use today. Jay Leno will frequently take his film team out into the street to quiz passers-by on some piece of knowledge related to science or history. He may ask, "Why does the sun rise in the east and set in the west?" The TV audience is then treated to a wide range of pre-Copernican explanations illustrating the apparent failure of education to teach the simplest principles of astronomy. Yet, the people who laughingly share their inaccurate knowledge are all well-dressed, obviously employed, happy, well-adjusted citizens. The fact that they do not know how the Earth rotates, that Togo is in Africa, or that humans have never seen a living dinosaur seems to have had little impact on their success. It would be nice if they knew these facts and concepts. In fact, they may, indeed, have learned them if their teachers had been able to teach them the richness of the concept rather than facts to be memorized for a test.

Large Idea!

We will need workers who can think outside the box, not people who can work in a straight row.

The school model that evolved out of the Industrial Age carried with it a fairly definite fingerprint of that time and its character. The wildly successful assembly line approach to producing goods manifested itself in our classrooms, where students moved from grade to grade, and teachers stood still in their classrooms installing mathematics on them, installing language arts, and the other components that would make a dependable Industrial Age employee. We had our blueprints and worked to make sure that all students matched the same specifications, that they all knew the same things, thought the same way, and were prepared to work in straight rows.

This model does not serve our children well today. In their future, it will not be what they know and how they think **alike** that will bring value to their endeavors. In the workplace of the twenty-first century it will be what they know that is **different**, how they think that is **different**, and how they perceive and solve problems **differently** that will accomplish goals. We will need workers who can think outside the box, not people who can work in a straight row. People who can unlearn and retool will be and remain economically viable contributors to their society.

The model for twentieth century education was highly linear. Students began in kindergarten or first grade and moved forward through the grades. At each stage of their development, new skills and knowledge were added to the assembly. The model in figure 5.3 illustrates a linear continuum of a student's education with the distinct and seldom integrated compartments of knowledge and skills.

The teacher delivered knowledge in the way that was most comfortable (lecture, handouts, worksheets, filmstrips), and the librarian maintained a library where students could check out books. Largely, the responsibility of learning was placed on the student, until the standards-based movement of the last decade.

The increasing challenges of living in a rapidly changing and information-driven world will certainly increase. We need to change our picture of education from one that produces a finished product, an educated person, to one that produces people who are able, willing, and eager to continue to learn in order to set and achieve goals. Education should identify the minimum knowledge that is required to build a context for the student and a foundation for further learning, and then facilitate the students' continued learning along desired and self-directed paths.

Establishing these foundation standards requires a willingness to ask some tough questions about what we learned in school and how we use it today. For instance, how many

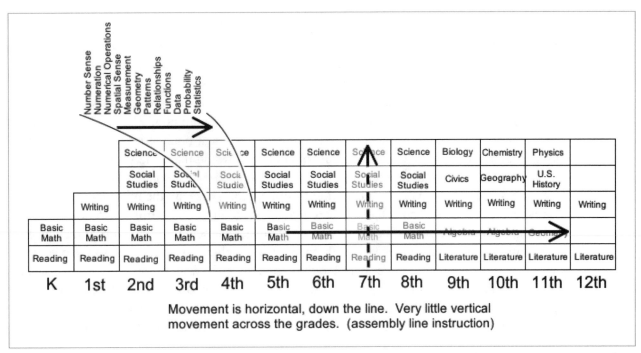

	Science	Science	Science	Science	Science	Science	Science	Biology	Chemistry	Physics	
	Social Studies	Social Studies	Social Studies	Social Studies	Social Studies	Social Studies	Social Studies	Civics	Geography	U.S. History	
Writing	Writing	Writing	Writing	Writing	Writing	Writing	Writing	Writing	Writing	Writing	Writing
Basic Math	Basic Math	Basic Math	Basic Math	Basic Math	Basic Math	Basic Math	Basic Math	Basic Math	Algebra	Algebra	Geometry	
Reading	Reading	Reading	Reading	Reading	Reading	Reading	Reading	Reading	Literature	Literature	Literature	Literature
K	1st	2nd	3rd	4th	5th	6th	7th	8th	9th	10th	11th	12th

Movement is horizontal, down the line. Very little vertical movement across the grades. (assembly line instruction)

Figure 5.3: Twentieth Century Education Model

long division problems have you performed on paper in the last month? If you did any division, it was probably with a four-dollar calculator. If you did a lot of dividing, you probably used a spreadsheet program. At the same time that we are doing less math on paper, our lives are probably impacted more by numbers than ever before. We are less aware of it because those numbers are being processed by computer, and not by hand. Our lives are driven by information, but we spend more of our time considering the information, evaluating its implication, and making goods that improve our own lives and the lives of others. Spending less time on the mechanics of calculation and more time learning to use the outcomes should be a goal of twenty-first century education.

When was the last time you had to balance a chemical formula, list the dates of the major battles of the American Civil War, perform a quadratic equation, label the bones of the human body, or name the major styles of art? These are all essential concepts to understand but only in as much as they combine to weave a rich context within which we all live. It has very little impact on anyone's future that every student can guarantee high standards of performance in all of these areas on a standardized test. It is important that students learn facts, but let us make sure that they are facts that they will actually need in their future. It is important that students learn about the world around them: local, global, large, small, personal, and communal. It is just as important that students leave their classrooms inspired to learn more about chemical reactions, anatomy, and the details of history. Forcing all students to memorize facts because it has always been done will not inspire.

Standards for the twenty-first century should comprise only the knowledge that creates a common context. It should instill in our students a sense of responsibility to family, friends, colleagues, neighbors, and fellow inhabitants of the planet—and to themselves. It should also awaken students to the enormous opportunities that are available to improve not only their lives, but the lives of others.

Standards should also reveal that these opportunities spring from a human story that is gloriously spiced by action, imagination, exploration, music, and imagery, all woven into its fabric, and that each of us is a character in that story. Students should also witness this story upon the stage of a natural environment that has enormous influence over our lives, and they should know that we exercise enormous influence over the natural environment. What students learn about their environment should lead them to appreciate the absolute wonder and miracle of life and existence and the beauty of its complexity. This is the context of our living, and it is a context that we should have in common.

Instead of moving along a linear continuum with clear boundaries between distinct disciplines, the twenty-first century model of education would place the student in the center of a sphere. Inside of that sphere, the student is surrounded by the context-building knowledge and skills that we will refer to as **foundation skills**. These are the minimum required competencies of our students, though there may be some differences from student to student. Sections of this layout would be fairly well distinguished as science, while others may be easily recognized as social studies, and still others would include basic mathematics. However, there would not be a hard border between these regions, they would flow fairly easily together in a way that reflects the integrated nature of these fields in the real world. This inner sphere of foundation skills would become richer as the students grow in age and learning, with distinctions between the disciplines becoming less apparent rather than more so.

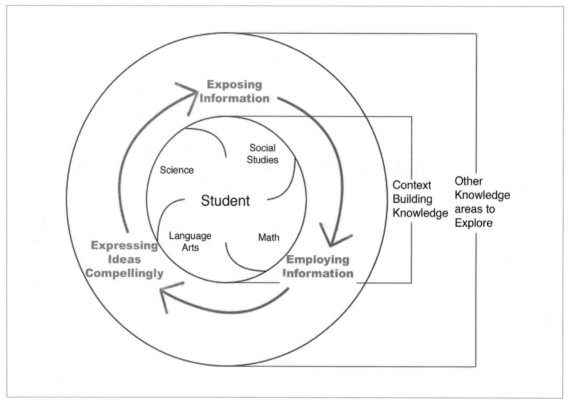

Figure 5.4: 21st Century Model — Part 1

Figure 5.4 illustrates this spherical model of education. It also shows how twenty-first century literacies are an integral part of the teaching and learning. In nearly all activities of learning, students would be utilizing techniques of finding information, decoding it, evaluating the information, organizing personal libraries of information, analyzing, processing, manipulating, and adding value to information, and expressing their growing understanding compellingly to others. These literacies of *exposing information, employing information*, and *expressing ideas compellingly* would float back and forth and up and down, as well as expand and contract, depending on the learning activity at hand.

The crucial part of education outside of twenty-first century literacies, and a shared context, is that students learn to teach themselves. This is why it is critical that all students be given more time to explore areas of special interest under the guidance of their teachers. Students should be expected to extend their knowledge into areas that are personally meaningful to them. It may be gene therapy, genealogy, geometry, or geology. It may be the American Civil War, the Civil Rights Movement, or Civil Disobedience. Their task, though, is to become an expert in that topic and to share their growing knowledge with others. They should research the topic, decode what they find, evaluate it to select the resources that are most valuable, analyze, manipulate, and assemble what they learn in a way that makes personal sense, and then create an information product that expresses their knowledge of the area in a way that compels other people.

The teacher's job, in supporting students' or teams' endeavors in extending their sphere, is to assist them by helping to move all of the literacies and various related fields of study toward their area of interest, and to help them to grasp the integrated nature of knowledge and the skills that leverage it. The library media specialist creates an information environment that helps students to become self-teachers and organizers of knowledge. The teacher and library media specialist become facilitators, though *consultant* may actually be a better term.

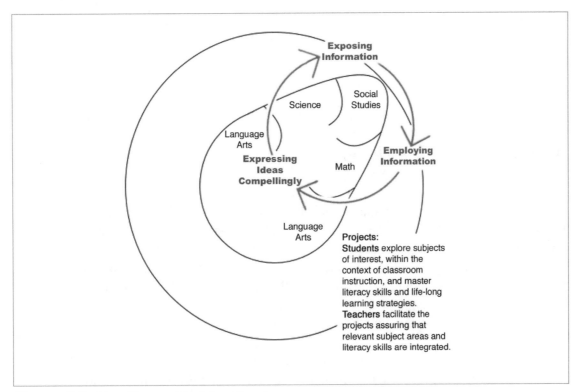

Figure 5.5: 21st Century Model — Part 2

Figure 5.5 illustrates how students will expand their knowledge beyond the foundation sphere. It is largely an act of self-teaching and reflects and supports lifelong learning practices. This aspect of the spherical education model is intended to echo real life-learning scenarios.

Characteristics of the future workplace that will certainly impact lifelong learning are teamwork and collaboration. These aspects can also be modeled in the classroom as interlocking spheres (figure 5.6), identifying topics in which groups of students express a common interest and then facilitating their work together.

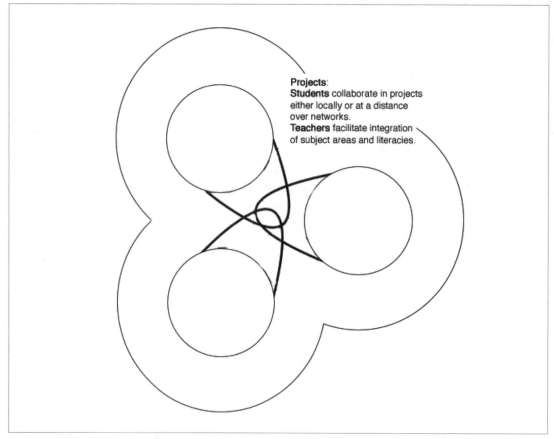

Projects:
Students collaborate in projects either locally or at a distance over networks.
Teachers facilitate integration of subject areas and literacies.

Figure 5.6: 21st Century Model — Part 3

Teachers and library media specialists support the students in their group endeavors by assuring that learning literacies are appropriately applied, that all related disciplines are leveraged, and that suitable resources are available and properly used.

Admittedly, this is not a model that fits well into today's institution of education. It requires an enormous amount of flexibility on the part of teachers and students, access to more information and communication technologies, and even a new school day schedule. The spherical model does assume three requirements in students:

1. Functional competence in twenty-first century literacy — the ability to find, access, decode, evaluate, manipulate, employ, and express information both digitally and in print.
2. Knowledge of the basic characteristics of our physical, social, and cultural environment both local and global to a degree that students are able to hold and convey a sense of who, when, and where they are in their world, how it impacts on them, and how their activities impact on it.

3. The ability to unlearn, self-teach, and make themselves experts in a variety of fields that the students find professionally and personally meaningful.

My first book was dedicated to Bill Edwards. His contributions to my learning and the education of thousands of other students in my small hometown bear repeating here. As in most high schools, we took elective courses in addition to our core classes. When I was a freshman, my small-town high school offered a limited number of electives. If you were in the band, you took band. If you were not in the band, you took industrial arts (shop). I took industrial arts, and Mr. Edwards was my shop teacher. Shop was an entirely different kind of class for me. First of all, there was no textbook. There were no activity sheets or other practice activities to hone specific skills and knowledge. Instead of teaching us isolated skills in order to cover the curriculum, he helped us to construct our own knowledge by helping us build something that might be used by someone. My project was to build a kayak. Other students built bookcases, lawn furniture, chessboards, and many other items. One team of students built a life-size replica of an Apollo space capsule and lived in it during one of the NASA flights.

As I consider what Mr. Edwards was doing, I realize that if he had taught us industrial arts skills in the same way that our other teachers were teaching information arts skills, he would have simply placed a stack of lumber on our desks and asked us to practice driving nails or put a stack of sheet metal on our desks and asked us to practice crimping the edges. He could have covered an entire curriculum if he had done it this way. Instead, each of us constructed our individual projects, mastering the associated skills and tools, and, as a result, built a context for industrial arts that applied directly to our personal experiences. He taught us to set goals, to ask questions of ourselves, and to make decisions that would accomplish our goals. He served us as a consultant rather than as a teacher, in the traditional sense. He was a facilitator of learning, and this style made perfect sense in teaching industrial arts skills during the Industrial Age. It makes just as much sense to teach information arts in this same way during the Information Age.

The cynical attitudes that are driving education reform today would say that teachers in the 1950s paid little attention to standardized test because they did not want to be held accountable, and that every minute our classes spent "off the subject" was time we were not spending on standards. The fact is that very little of the knowledge I use today in my day-to-day work even existed in the 1950s and '60s, and the belief that we can accurately define the knowledge that our children will use 20 years from now is arrogant at best.

Action Items

Directors of Technology

- Consider renaming your Acceptable Use Policy (AUP) to Ethics in Information Policy (EIP). Expand this document to include the ethical use of all information and information processing and delivery technologies.
- Consider establishing an EIP that is meaningful at an elementary-school level, one for the middle school, and one for high schools. You might even consider a separate EIP for staff.
- Work toward describing elements of the EIP as proactive ways of promoting meaningful use of technology, rather than exclusively in terms of limiting access. Think in terms of "Thou shall …" rather than "thou shall not …"

- Work with the central office supervisors of other content areas to integrate EIP practices into their curriculum work and professional development endeavors.
- Try to limit your use of the term *technology* when discussing integration, staff development, and planning. Try to use the term *literacy* as much as possible and utilize all opportunities to help people to understand a different vision or definition of what literacy is for our students.
- Establish staff development for teachers aimed at critical evaluation of Net-based and other information sources.

Principals

- Make sure that the entire faculty understands the district's EIP or AUP and that all teachers are making their students clearly aware of their opportunities, responsibilities, and limitations.
- Make sure, during casual and formal evaluations, that all teachers are making use of a variety of information resources, and that they are encouraging students to question the ethical use of information sources that are available to them.

Media Specialists

- Add a page to your media center Web site that points to Web tools designed to assist students (and teachers) in evaluating information resources and in crediting the owners/authors of the information. (There are examples on this book's Web site at <http://landmark-project.com/redefining_literacy>.)
- Provide casual professional development for teachers in evaluating and crediting information from the Internet and other resources.
- Work with students to make sure that they understand how to evaluate and credit information resources.

School Tech Facilitators

- Assist the media specialist in establishing a Web page with links to Web tools designed to assist students (and teachers) in evaluating information resources and in crediting the owners/authors of the information.
- Provide other casual and formal professional development on evaluating and crediting information sources.
- Organize technology fairs for parents and community members and use these opportunities to, among other things, help people understand that the value of information is changing, and, as a result, ethical issues need to be addressed.

Teachers

- Require that students cite all unoriginal information that is used in their information products.
- Require that students evaluate all unoriginal information that is used in their information products.

■ Be willing to put students' selected information sources on trial, asking students to defend their usage of the information.

Students

■ The information that you use to learn and to communicate is only as valuable as its truthfulness. Make sure it is truthful.

Parents

■ Ask your children about information they find on the Internet or in magazines and reference books. Ask them why they think it is true and what the implications might be if it is not.

Conclusion!
A Student of the Future

Several years ago I worked as a consultant for ThinkQuest, an educational project created by Advanced Network and Services. Al Weis, the organization's president, wanted to create an opportunity for students to learn not only technical skills associated with the growing Internet, but also to learn other disciplines within an increasingly digital and connected world.

ThinkQuest was a revolutionary project because, in 1995, most teachers had not heard of the World Wide Web. It was a contest between teams of students who created Web sites and competed for scholarships and fame. However, at a deeper and more relevant level, ThinkQuest was an experience within which students explored and mastered twenty-first century literacy. They learned to expose information: find relevant information, decode it, and evaluate it to determine its value. They learned to employ their information: analyzing, processing, manipulating, and adding value to the knowledge they gained. Finally, these teams of students learned to express their ideas compellingly through text, images, virtual reality, sound, and video.

Each year, Advanced Network & Services held a ThinkQuest weekend where a final level of judging took place and the final awards were presented—more than a million dollars in scholarships. In my association with ThinkQuest, I was able to attend a number of these events, each in a major city. At the end of the second year, the culminating event was held in Washington, D.C. On the second afternoon, each team was provided with a state-of-the-art computer and high-speed connection to the Internet and was asked to demonstrate and discuss its Web site with visitors from across the city. It was highly illuminating to see what these high-school students had learned in the process. Everyone was appropriately impressed with these accomplishments. By the end of the afternoon, I had visited and spoken with most of the teams, but just before leaving, I noticed a computer in the corner with a poster above it that displayed in gothic script The Middle Ages.

There was only one young man at the computer. His partners had obviously left since it was the end of the session. I walked over to the young man ready to talk some history. After all, I had taught history for nearly 10 years, and I thought I would educate him a bit. As it turned out, he educated me—a humbling experience. What amazed me about this young man's knowledge was not the command he had of the major events of those centuries, but what he had learned about the nuances of their lifestyles: how people had fun, the work they did, their festivals, how the castes interacted with each other, and more.

I finally asked the youngster how old he was, and he responded, "15." Then I asked where he had learned about the Middle Ages, to which he responded, "from college professors".

I asked again how old he was, just in case I had misunderstood. Finding that I had not, I asked how he had arranged to learn about the Middle Ages from college professors. He then explained that when he had identified what he needed to learn, he would visit university Web sites and look for courses that probably taught it. Then he would send an e-mail message to the professor of the course, asking questions that would evoke the answers he needed. The boy then explained that he never told the professor that he was 15 years old. He said that he was a graduate assistant doing research.

As I finally walked away from this student, his teacher caught up with me and explained that the young man I had been talking to was not a successful student, that he had been at risk of failing core subjects, and that he had a generally poor attitude about school. She explained that he had blossomed as a result of this project and had exhibited not only an eagerness to learn, but also leadership skills that had never been apparent before.

It is my opinion that what this young man learned as a result of his participation in ThinkQuest was as important, if not more so, than what his classmates who were making good grades were learning. This young man had learned to make himself an expert, and he and his classmates will be doing this for the rest of their lives. If our children are ready for the twenty-first century, it is because they know how to teach themselves. At the heart of being lifelong self-educating people is a literacy that is relevant to the time and the information that surrounds them. It means that they cannot only read the information that someone hands to them, but that they can investigate and expose the truth behind that information. It means that they can count, measure, calculate numbers, but it also means that they can employ the information that they have found to solve problems, accomplish goals, and add to their experience. Not only can they write, but they can also express their ideas in ways that affect other people using images, animation, sound, and video.

Finally, lifelong learners must know how to use information responsibly and within a context that is shared by other people. In a world that is increasing driven by information, the ethical use of information is key to helping our friends, communities, and world to improve the world's condition.

Now it is your turn. I have given you a variety of suggestions, or action items to consider in your own working environment. These are suggestions for ways that various stakeholders might further the modernization of schools and classrooms. Consider them and use those that fit well with your circumstances.

I also want to urge you to talk back to me and other readers of this book. Go to the Web site at <http://landmark-project.com/redefining_literacy/>. You will be able to comment on aspects of this book that impress you in some way and discuss with others and me where we might go to further promote a new literacy for the twenty-first century.

Thank you!

Works Cited

Boese, Christine. "To Blog or not to Blog." *CNN Headline News*. 23 September 2002. Retrieved 5 May 2003 <http://www.cnn.com/2002/SHOWBIZ/09/20/hln.hot.buzz.blog/>.

"How Much Information." *School of Information Management & Systems*. 2000. Regents of the University of California. 13 March 2001 <http://www.sims.berkeley.edu/how-much-info/summary.html>.

James, Jennifer. *Thinking in the Future Tense: Leadership for a New Age*. 2002 Technology Leadership Academy. Pennsylvania Department of Education. The Penn Stater Conference Center Hotel, Pennsylvania. 9 July 2002.

McCarthy, Wil. "Ultimate Alchemy." *WIRED Magazine Archives*. October 2001. Retrieved 31 August 2003 <http://www.wired.com/wired/archive/9.10/atoms_pr.html>.

"Microsoft Reader with ClearType—Time line." *Microsoft Corporation*. 01 May 2003 <http://www.microsoft.com/READER/press/time line_future.htm>.

Mokhoff, Nicolas. "Old Models Can't Explain New Economy, Speaker Says." *EE Times*. 10/31/00. CMP Media, Inc. 25 November 2000 <http://www.eetimes.com/story/OEG20001031S0022>.

Rideout, Victoria, Caroline Richardson, and Paul Resnick. "See No Evil: How Internet Filters Affect the Search for Online Health Information." *The Henry J. Kaiser Family Foundation*. 18 February 2003 <http://www.kff.org/content/2002/3294/Internet_Filtering_exec_summ.pdf>.

Scheeres, Julia. "Latin America: the Mobile World." Wired News. (2001). 8 September 2003 <http://www.wired.com/news/technology/0,1282,41309,00.html>.

Shachtman, Noah. "It's Teleportation—For Real." *Wired News*. (2001). 4 January 2003 <http://www.wired.com/news/technology/0,1282,47191,00.html>.

"SLAC Scientists Help Set Data Transfer Speed Record." *Stanford Linear Accelerator Center SLAC*. 06 May 2003 <http://www.slac.stanford.edu/slac/media-info/20030207/>.

Sullivan, Danny. "Direct Navigation to Sites Rules, But Search Engines Remain Important." *Search Engine Watch* Jupitermedia Corporation. 07 January 2003 <http://www.searchenginewatch.com/sereport/02/02-nav.html>.

Warlick, Ryann. Personal Interview. 13 March 2003.

Appendix A

Other Suggested Works—Books

Adolescents and Literacies in a Digital World (*New Literacies and Digital Epistemologies*, Vol. 7). Ed. Donna E. Alvermann. Peter Lang Publishing. 2002. ISBN 0820455733

Being Digital. Nicolas Negroponte. Alfred A. Knopf. 1995. ISBN 0679762906

Beyond Technology: Questioning, Research and the Information Literate School. Jamie McKenzie. FNO Press. 2000. ISBN 0967407826

Catalog of Tomorrow: Trends Shaping your Future. Ed. Andrew Zolli. TechTV. 2002. ISBN 0789728109

Digital Literacy. Paul Gilster. John Wiley & Sons. 1997. ISBN 0471165204

The Director in the Classroom. Nikos Theodosakis. Tech4Learning, Inc. 2001. ISBN 1930870116

Empowering Students with Technology. Alan November. Skylight Publishing. 2001. ISBN 1575173727

Ethics in School Librarianship. Carol Simpson. Linworth Publishing. 2003. ISBN 1586830848

Growing Up Digital. Don Tapscot. McGraw-Hill Trade. 1999. ISBN 0071347984

Learning Right from Wrong in the Digital Age: An Ethics Guide for Parents, Teachers, Librarians, and Others Who Care About Computer-Using Young People. Doug Johnson. Linworth Publishing Company. 2003. ISBN 1586831313

Literacy in a Digital World: Teaching and Learning in the Age of Information. Kathleen Tyner. Lawrence Erlbaum Assoc. 1998. ISBN 0805822267

Millennials Rising. Neil Howe & William Strauss. Vintage Books. 2000. ISBN 0375707190

The Next Fifty Years: Science in the First Half of the 21st Century. Ed. John Brockman. Vintage Books. 2002. ISBN 0375713425

Teaching TV Production in a Digital World: Integrating Media Literacy. Robert Kenny. Libraries Unlimited. 2001. ISBN 156308726X

Thinking in the Future Tense. Jennifer James. Free Press. 1997. ISBN 0684832690

Other Suggested Works—Web Documents

"Digital Literacy: Re-Thinking Education and Training in a Digital World."
<http://digitalliteracy.mwg.org/>

"Digital Transformation A Framework for ICT Literacy"
<http://www.ets.org/search97cgi/s97_cgi>

"The Importance of Contemporary Literacy in the Digital Age: A Response to Digital Transformation: A Framework for ICT Literacy"
<http://www.cosn.org/resources/051402.htm>

The Literacy Web (at the University of Connecticut)
<http://www.literacy.uconn.edu/>
"More than Access."
<http://www.educause.edu/pub/er/erm00/articles006/erm0063.pdf>
"A New Digital Literacy: A Conversation with Paul Gilster."
<http://www.ascd.org/readingroom/edlead/9711/pool.html>
"A Primer on Digital Literacy."
<http://horizon.unc.edu/projects/resources/digital_literacy.asp>
"Report: Digital literacy is essential for students."
<http://www.eschoolnews.com/news/showStory.cfm?ArticleID=3592>

Appendix B

Where to Look to Find the Future

The Harrow Group
<http://www.theharrowgroup.com/>
The Media Lab
<http://www.media.mit.edu/>
Xerox PARC
<http://www.parc.xerox.com/>
Institute of NanoTechnology
<http://www.nano.org.uk/>
IBM Research
<http://researchweb.watson.ibm.com/>
Technology Review
<http://www.technologyreview.com/>
SlashDot: News for Nerds
<http://slashdot.org/>
TechDirt
<http://www.techdirt.com>
SciTech
<http://www.scitech.com>

Appendix C

Designing information for scanning

Investigative Strategies — Finding Evidence

If I were to continue our field trip through th[...]ld of networked information, the next major achi[...] [earch] Engine. These powerful and immensel[...] search for information through enormous on[...]h billions of Web documents for specific [...] seemingly magical tools at our disposal, it [...] actly what is happening when we use[...]es on a given topic.

(Speech bubble: Headings & subheadings are arranged as hanging indents to make them easier to find by scanning the pages.)

What Search Engines Do

First of all, search engines do not search the Internet, at least in the way that you might suspect. When searching a book for the answer to your [...]estion, you rarely scan the entire book. You scan the table of contents [...] ndex for references to the problem. Search engines also search [...]es to find references to Web pages. These indexes can be huge, [...]g references to billions of Web pages, as is the case with **Google** [...]tp://www.google.com>).

(Speech bubble: Content is indented, shortening the lines, making the text easier to read.)

The indexes of other search engines can be small. Yahoo's directory index represents only a tiny fraction of what Google has. However, this does not mean that Google is better than Yahoo. It means that they enable us to solve different kinds of problems. Sometimes it is more suitable to deal with 200 hits than with 400,000 hits.

Search Engine Vocabulary

Search Engine   A search engine scans an index for web pages that include the words or phrases described in the search phrase.

Web Directory   A web directory arranges web pages from its index into a [...]cading series of menus, starting with general subjects, linking [...] highly spec[...]

Index Size   Indicates the am[...] [...]sented by the index, reflected by the n[...] et. Large index search engines are not ne[...] small index search engines.

(Speech bubble: Arrange all lists in tables or bulleted lists.)

Relevancy Ranking	This is how the search engine arranges the hits, identifying those web pages that are probably most relevant to the problem you are trying to solve. There are a variety of ways to do this including: number of occurrences of the keyword, where the keyword appears in the web page, whether the keyword is in the page title, other web pages that link to the considered page.
Freshness	How quickly the search engine is able to find and include new web pages. This will indicate how current the hits will be.
Boolean	A language for posting questions to a search engine. Involves connectors and punctuation to describe relationships between words in the search phrase.

It is also helpful to understand that most search engines create their own indexes. If we had to rely on people to add all of the Web pages to a search engine's index, we would be woefully behind in representing the content of the Internet in our Web searches.

These enormous indexes are grown and maintained by semi-intelligent software agents. Before your imagination takes over, let me explain that these agents, often called spiders, are merely small pieces of software that are programmed to wander through the WWW, following Web links in much the same way that you browse through links as you surf the Net. These spider programs record the links that they encounter and when they find a hyperlink that has not been recorded, they follow it to its target page. The spider then checks the page to see if it is already known by the search. If not, the spider sends all of the pertinent information about the page back to the search engine, where it is added to the index.

What We Do in Searching for Information

This is an important concept to understand, because it explains why, when you use a search engine, you often receive a large number of hits that seem to be completely unrelated to your topic. Search engines are wonderfully powerful tools. But they cannot think. They search for strings of characters, not meaning. They do the best that they can to put the most relevant pages at the top of your list of hits, but they do not truly understand what you want.

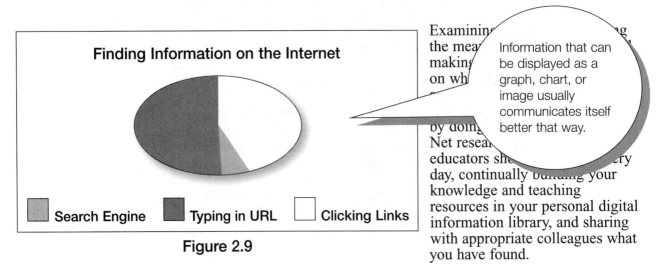

Examining the meaning, making on wh... by doing Net resea... educators sh... ry day, continually building your knowledge and teaching resources in your personal digital information library, and sharing with appropriate colleagues what you have found.

Information that can be displayed as a graph, chart, or image usually communicates itself better that way.

Finding Information on the Internet

Search Engine   Typing in URL   Clicking Links

Figure 2.9

The truth is that search engines are a surprisingly underutilized tool. According to Danny Sullivan of Search Engine Watch, only 7 to 8 percent of Web destinations are reached using a search engine. (See figure 2.9) By comparison, 52% are reached by entering the URL, and 41% by clicking links. (<http://www.searchenginewatch.com/sereport/02/02-nav.html>) This indicates that there is a great deal of valuable information that is not being used, because people do not understand or use search engines. Much more information about these tools and their use can be found at two rich Web sites: **Search Engine Watch** (<http://www.searchenginewatch.com>) and **Search Engine Showdown** (<http://www.searchengineshowdown.com>).

Most of the readers of this book have used search engines to find information on the Internet. You have typed keywords into your favorite search engine and then scanned through the first 20 or 30 Web sites out of the tens or hundreds of thousands of hits. Or you may simply look at of the first five or six pages that appear in the list. So you may even be improving your results by using Boolean or proximity your search phrases. The strategy of searching the Net is much deeper than knowing when to use AND, OR, and NOT.

> When the style of information changes, communicate it to the glancing eye by changing the style of the text.

A Student Scenario

I am going to describe this strategy. But first, we will walk through a scenario of a middle school student conducting Internet research in order to complete an assignment. Her name is Suzette, and her teacher has given her class the following assignment.

> *It is 2050 and we are terraforming the planet Mars. Scientists are identifying animals from our planet to migrate to Mars and are especially interested in grazing animals. Your assignment is to select a grazing animal and submit a report that describes the animal and how it interacts with other organisms in its ecosystem.*

Suzette has two problems:

1. Select a grazing animal for her report.

2. Collect information about the animal and how it interacts with other organisms.

> Display ordered lists with numbers.

She starts, as most of us do, with a large search engine such as Google, entering *grazing animals* as her search phrase. She receives 280,000 hits. She scans the first page or two and finds Web sites on grazing terminology, official documents of the Environmental Protection Agency, and books on the management of domestic farm animals in The Netherlands. Although some of these pages might be helpful later, they do not help Suzette with her first problem, selecting a grazing animal.